# IT
## MUST BE
### FIVE O'
### CLOCK
### SOME-
### WHERE

SYLVIA CARY

*When you're in the happiness business, nothing can go wrong— can it?*

Jo Sue P. & Kelly —
Hope you enjoy
my journey — &
your own !
Best, Sylvia Cary

CompCare Publications
2415 Annapolis Lane
Minneapolis, Minnesota 55441

Cary, Sylvia.
    It must be five o'clock somewhere.

    Autobiographical.
    1. Cary, Sylvia—Mental health. 2. Alcoholism—Patients—United States—Biography. 3. Psychologists—United States—Biography.    I. Title.
RC565.C39 1986      616.86′1′00924 [B]      86-4199
ISBN 0-89638-099-8
ISBN 0-89638-094-7 (pbk.)

Cover design by Lillian E. Svec

    Inquiries, orders, and catalog requests should be addressed to
    CompCare Publications
    2415 Annapolis Lane
    Minneapolis, Minnesota 55441
    Call toll free 800/328/3330
    (Minnesota residents 559-4800)

1      2      3      4      5      6      7      8      9

86               87               88               89               90

To
Lance
Jessica and Claudia
Dick
Evie
Marion W., Nancy C.,
Jack K., and Keven B.

"Every one of these hundreds of millions of human beings is in some form seeking happiness...Not one is altogether noble nor altogether trustworthy nor altogether consistent, and not one is altogether vile...Not a single one but has at some time wept."

H. G. Wells, *The Outline of History*

# – 1 –

# A CLOUD ON THE HORIZON
# AS BIG AS A FIST

*Luck is when the guy next to you gets hit with the arrow.*
*—Aristotle, quoted by Ernest Becker*
The Denial of Death

Sandy must have had misgivings. He was a nailbiter anyway, but today he was worse. All the way into Manhattan for the wedding he chewed on the cuticles of his left hand and steered the new black Thunderbird convertible with his right. An unfiltered Camel cigarette was between his fingers.

He took a deep drag.

"Sanford, you're oral," I said.

"No shit."

How fitting to be marrying a psychiatrist. I don't mean because I was in the mental health business myself, but because I was marrying into the family religion—Orthodox Freudian. I was already the third generation of Carys to hightail it into the city on the commuter train for appointments with what my mother used to call "the dentist."

My grandfather (who was known to be *avant garde*) had started it all by grabbing himself one of the first Viennese psychoanalysts off the boat. In no time he was lying on a brand new couch from Bloomingdale's and free-associating his heart out—even before Herr Doctor had learned to understand English. No matter. My grandfather got better anyway, which tells you something.

In our family we went to psychiatrists for the same reasons some people go to church—to get the answers to the things that hurt. The path to happiness was seen as winding its way *inward*, not *upward*.

1

And just as you wouldn't expect another Catholic to tell you what he or she had dealt with in confession, we didn't presume to inquire about each other's neuroses: "Don't tell *me* about it, Sylvie. Save it for your appointment with Dr. X," my mother would say when I started to spill out my feelings to her in the kitchen.

"Oh, I forgot."

This February day, our wedding day, was overcast with the smell of snow in the air. But I love gloomy weather; it makes me cheerful. The trees along the Connecticut turnpike were bare and silvery grey, quite a contrast to the brilliant colors of all the flowers in the back seat that we were bringing with us for the ceremony. The car heater warmed my toes. I felt happy. I was where I wanted to be. I was about to marry the man I wanted to marry this time. I had no conscious fears about marriage or about how I'd do at this thing ahead of me called life.

I had thumbed through the Jewish books that Sandy's mother and her rabbi decided I should read before the ceremony. Not being Jewish, I worried them and they figured the books might help me understand Sandy better. But Sandy had little interest in being Jewish and even less interest in being understood. I used to think of him as the John Wayne of mental health.

Yet here he was, puffing away on his cigarette and chewing on his nails, about to give up his independence for me.

No wonder he had misgivings.

Would we be happy?

I studied him a minute, what I could see of him through the Camel smoke. I looked at his soft hazel eyes, his silky brown hair, sensuous mouth and perfect profile, then decided he was too cute to give me trouble. If there was going to be any trouble in *this* marriage, it was going to have to come from me.

My aunt and uncle's East 74th Street apartment was warm and full of the odors of the upcoming wedding supper. Sandy and I stood just inside the front door accepting hugs and greetings. The doorman was at our heels, smiling, arms full of flowers. He reminded me of the charming old elevator man in the building where I grew up. Once, somewhere between the lobby and the sixth floor, he exposed himself to me. For the next year and a half I walked up and down six flights of stairs just to avoid the risk of being alone with him again.

It never occurred to me to tell anybody.

"Happy wedding day, Sylvie!" said my Aunt Ramona, bending down to give me a kiss on the cheek. She was the tallest woman in our family.

2

I recognized a husky laugh from the other side of the room. It was Faye, Sandy's sister.

Faye had a nasty drinking problem, which was currently causing a lot of uproar in the family. Sandy did what he could to ignore Faye, which made Faye all the more desperate. She wanted Sandy to worship her again—the way he did when he was three and she was six.

Faye was perched on the edge of the piano bench, Scotch in hand. She was talking to the husband of my matron of honor. From the look on his face he was just beginning to catch on that she wasn't making sense. She was wearing a brown silk dress and the same strand of cultured pearls that had once led Sandy to make a crack the family still relished repeating: "Those pearls sure as hell didn't get cultured hanging around *her* neck!"

My sister Justine was on the couch in an intense (probably political) discussion with an equally intense male cousin. She was in her last year of high school and into her hippy-liberal-scruffy phase—long blond hair rather tangled and no makeup. Even though years younger, she was the first one of the two of us to get published and the first to smoke grass.

Behind her, serving cheese and crackers, was my mother Bonnie, a good-looking woman. Her cornflower blue eyes were dramatized by a dress the same color.

I inherited my mother's looks and dark hair, but not her cornflower eyes. Mine are chameleon eyes that change from grey to slate blue or green depending on what I'm wearing and maybe even the weather.

She smiled. She was a lot happier about this wedding than my last one to an Austrian violinist nearly fifteen years my senior. I think I fell in love with the fact that he spoke five languages and had actually seen Hitler. Somehow I thought if I married him I'd take on his experiences as well as his name—or as a friend later cracked, "Don't develop it, marry it."

For the two years Lucas and I were together, my mother was a model of restraint, keeping her distaste for him to herself. But once she lost control of herself. I'd been boasting about how Lucas had been a child prodigy and she shot out: "He still *is!*" She clapped her hand over her mouth in horror and apologized.

She never wanted to do anything that interfered with what I thought I wanted, even if what I wanted was ridiculous. First of all, she knew I was a willful character and it probably wouldn't have done any good. Secondly, she figured falling on my face was a good way for me to learn.

3

Besides, that's exactly how I operate.

"You're amazing," Sandy said to me years later. "When you walk into a wall, you pick yourself up, brush yourself off—and walk right back into another wall!"

I noticed Walt, my stepfather, standing near the fish tank, talking to Sandy's best man, Ed (also a psychiatrist), and gesturing with his beautiful hands. Justine and I were both in love with Walt's hands. One of the best things either of us could say about a new man was: "He's got Daddy's hands!"

A few other wedding guests were hovering near Walt's conversation, listening. I smiled. That was definitely Walt's way. He created an instant "literary salon" wherever he went and could always be found in a corner discussing something he'd just read a piece on in *The New Yorker* or the *New York Times*. When I was a kid I loved having him at my parties because he made conversations so easy for my friends. He'd ask marvelous questions and give instant feedback: "Ah-hah! What an interesting thought!" They loved it. He made them feel grown up.

His favorite discussion topic was psychiatry. It was his passion. At home in Connecticut his downstairs office was lined with shelves of books on mental health. He had stacks of psychiatric and psychoanalytic journals everywhere. Piles of newspaper clippings cluttered his desk. My mother was always shutting his office door so she wouldn't have to look at any of it.

"You'd think some old eccentric lived in there," she'd say.

It was Walt, of course, who first introduced me to Sigmund Freud and was responsible for my going to a few of those New York "dentists" myself (starting at age eight) and for becoming a psychotherapist later on.

In junior high school he gave me a book called *A Young Person's Guide to Freud* which I read boldly in study hall feeling pretty *avant garde* too.

Walt waved Sandy and me over to his little fish tank salon.

"Sylvie-Sylvie! Sandy! Come here a sec'." We walked over. Sandy shook Ed's hand and Walt gave me a big squeezy hug. "I was just talking to Ed here about the Ernest Jones biography of Freud. I've just read volume three. Have you read it yet, Sandy?"

Sandy shook his head.

"Ah, too bad. It's a crackerjack job."

He was about to launch into a more detailed review of the work when we were interrupted by Sandy's mother, Hedy. She had a preoccupied, non-festive look on her face.

"Sanford!" She clutched his arm. "Your goddamned sister's had too much to drink again."

"She's drunk," Sandy corrected.

"Well, whatever. Will you talk to her?"

"And say what?"

"Hell, I don't know! *You're* the psychiatrist. You know what to say."

This was promising to get a little exciting!

The adrenaline started coursing through my veins. Drama. I loved it. I loved it when Faye's drinking got negative attention. Whenever she drank, she got so outrageously obnoxious that I always looked adorable by comparison, like a darling. And if there was one thing I liked, it was looking like a darling.

I glanced over at "poor Faye" who was weaving on the edge of the piano bench.

Well, I thought, if somebody's got to get hit with Aristotle's arrow—better Faye than me!

Sandy headed off across the room to talk to his sister, which in itself surprised me. Usually a direct request like Hedy's brought out the rebel in Sandy. He'd dig in and refuse to budge—the "anal retentive" part of his nature, I'd tell him.

But today he gave in like a lamb.

Faye saw him coming. "Sandy baby!" She clunked her wet glass down on the piano's polished wood surface, and stretched her arms out towards Sandy, who quickly grabbed them to keep Faye from enveloping him. He gave her a restrained peck on the cheek.

"You're late, baby!" she said in a loud, thick voice. "We were all getting so worried about you. We thought you might have had an *accident*."

At that precise second I caught my mother's eye; she winked at me and we both giggled. It was an inside joke. Only psychiatrically-oriented sophisticates (like us, of course) understood that someone who worries about someone else having an accident probably has unconscious hostility towards them.    What "poor Faye" had just done was to tell a room full of people that she hated her brother—at least *unconsciously*.

5

I was embarrassed for her. I couldn't think of anything worse than getting caught with my unconscious flapping out there in the breeze for all to see. In my own life I tried to make sure this never happened. I reviewed and rehearsed things before I said them. I never told dreams in public. I was on guard against "Freudian slips." And if I did make a slip, I had a couple of explanations memorized to get me out of it. Sometimes I found it was better just to listen and let other people do the talking.

Of course, all this had a certain impact upon my spontaneity, but I figured it was a small price to avoid looking bad.

Faye went right on babbling, oblivious to the fact that she'd just embarrassed herself. Miraculously, Sandy got her to lower her voice. And whatever it was he said to her left her smiling. Then he walked back towards us.

Hedy was impressed. "My-my, what on earth did you *tell* her, Sanford? She looks so pleased."

"I told her I'd go get her another drink."

Hedy was irritated. "I was hoping for something a little more *psychiatric,*" she said to me as Sandy walked off. "He didn't have to go through medical school just to come up with *that!*"

It was getting late, past the time we'd set to be married, but somehow I couldn't get around to giving the signal to begin. I caught the rabbi looking at his watch. I knew I was into my procrastination nonsense again, dilly-dallying on purpose—partly because it made me feel in control.

I stopped to talk to Rosie, my matron of honor. We'd met in graduate school in Boston. All year long I'd nagged her to stick it out. She'd just married a man in the carpet business and all she wanted to do was stay home and play house.

"Finish the year, you idiot!" I kept telling her. "If you don't you'll be sorry." What I didn't want to say out loud was that any marriage to a man who only sold rugs was doomed. She'd be on her own in no time, so she'd better have a graduate degree.

"I'm so nervous about this marriage I could plotz," Rosie said to me. "You have to promise me you'll never get divorced!" She and Dave had introduced me to Sandy; now she felt responsible for the results, especially since I wasn't Jewish.

"Don't worry," I said. "No chance." I gave her a hug. "I'd better go get dressed."

In the bathroom I closed the door and sat down on the edge of the cool tub, suddenly wanting to be alone and disappear. When I was a kid at the lake I used to like to go under the water and hold my breath until they'd worry and start calling me. Then I'd surface in a huge splash.

"Here I am!"

The day I married Lucas in Connecticut, I disappeared for two hours up on the hill behind the house. I sat on a rock and listened to the sounds of people looking for me: "Sylvie! SYLVIE! SYL-VI-AH!" Finally, when I was ready to be found I shouted back: "Here I am, up here on the hill!"

And now I was sitting on the edge of the tub with my eyes closed, disappearing into myself. I went inward so fast and so deep that for a split second I saw how a person could do this and never come back.

That scared me. My eyes flew open when I heard my mother calling me.

"Here I am! I'm in here! I'm in the bathroom! Can you hear me?"

"Sylvie, are you okay?"

"Sure, I'll be right out."

"You need any help?"

"No."

"Call me if you do."

Standing there in front of the rabbi between two flower-covered grand pianos wasn't as easy as I thought it would be. My legs shook, my heart pounded in my ears.

Sandy and I had worked hard on the words of the ceremony—no mention of God, "husband and wife" instead of "man and wife," scratch the word "obey"—and add some other stuff. Now it was all being said and I couldn't listen. I was worried about missing a cue or saying the wrong line. I was worried about looking bad.

I shouldn't have worried. Faye did it for me. Just as the rabbi was saying "I now pronounce you husband and wife," Faye, with her characteristic bad timing, stepped on his line:

"Bravo!!" she shouted.

The rabbi winced, but he quickly got the spotlight back onto us when he tossed something at Sandy's feet. I jumped, startled. Sandy knew exactly what to do—he stomped on it.

For a minute I didn't know what was happening. Then I remembered it was what Sandy called "the old glass in the sock trick." It was a

7

custom I'd read about in one of those books I'd been flipping through earlier on the way into town.

Sandy leaned towards me for the wedding kiss.

It was done. We were married. There was a gold ring on my finger and a matching one on Sandy's. There was clapping. There were hugs.

And the party began.

Maids burst forth from the kitchen like dancers, carrying trays of champagne. My Aunt Ramona began bringing in the food and my Uncle Hal sat down at one of the pianos and launched into a Strauss waltz.

Walt danced me around the living room, champagne glass in hand, careful to avoid knocking us into Uncle Hal's Ming horse which stood (heavily insured) on a stand. He was smiling and openly proud of me.

"My Sylvie-Sylvie!" he kept saying. "What a grand day!"

Suddenly there was an explosive crack! The Ming horse shivered and the fish in the tank darted for cover. The music, the talking, the waltzing stopped. Nobody spoke. We all looked in the direction of the noise—the front door.

Hedy cleared her throat; she looked uncomfortable.

"That was *Faye,*" she explained. "She had to leave."

A few looks went back and forth—and then we all got back to business.

"Faye does that," I said to Walt as we resumed our dance. "She's got a terrible drinking problem. But sometimes, just minutes before she turns into a werewolf, she splits—like she knows when it's coming on. Sandy and I call it 'Faye's rays.' Anyway, thank God for Faye's rays tonight. She's a bitch on wheels when she's drunk."

"Is she doing anything about it?"

"Doing something about it" meant, of course, seeing a psychiatrist or psychoanalyst. That was the answer for just about every other kind of human problem, so it was probably the answer for a drinking problem too.

"No," I said, "she's resistant."

"Ah, too bad. If she's drinking too much she needs some help to find out *why* so she can stop."

"But Daddy, then we wouldn't all have somebody to talk about!"

We both laughed.

When a tray of champagne floated by, Walt took two glasses— another for himself and one for me. Sandy, now at my elbow, took one too.

I drank my whole glass down at once.

"God, don't *gulp* that stuff!" Sandy said.

For an instant, without warning, I felt a surge of fury. How dare he watch me!

"I was thirsty," I said defensively. I wasn't really thirsty. I didn't even know why I gulped it.

And then, just as quickly as the feeling came it left. I snapped back to normal.

Walt raised his glass to the room: "A toast! A TOAST!"

Everyone stopped to pay attention.

"A toast to Sanford and Sylvie—two beautiful and talented therapists who are now united in marriage and love. Together they'll work, side by side, equal in all things, to bring better mental health to a world that sure as hell can use it!"

Sandy raised his glass. There was a mischievous look in his eye. "Work as equals, side by side, eh? You mean just like Madame Curie and What's-his-name?"

Sandy's crack, delivered in his usual dry style, made everyone laugh and dissolved any remaining tension over Faye's abrupt departure.

I laughed too. I snuggled up close to Sandy and he put his arm around me.

"Let's be happy, okay?" Sandy said to me. There was just a touch of tentativeness in his voice.

I smiled at him reassuringly. "That's easy."

# – 2 –

# FORK IN THE ROAD

*If we do not change our direction, we are likely to end up where we are headed.*
—*Old Chinese proverb*

The blizzard hit the day after the wedding as we headed north towards Vermont and our ski resort honeymoon. The Thunderbird rattled and shook in the wind, the heater going full blast. I was wearing my fur coat from Filene's in Boston and my black sheepskin fur hat from Gumm's in Moscow. Lucas had bought it for me when he was there on tour.

I had a slight headache from the wedding champagne, which made me think of Faye and her drunken exit from the reception.

"I'm surprised Faye didn't call us this morning and apologize," I said to Sandy, trying to disguise the criticism in my voice that even I could detect. "She *knew* where we were staying."

"That's assuming she even remembers last night," Sandy said.

"How could anyone forget a thing like that?"

During the night the temperature slid down to zero and froze the snow onto the branches of all the trees. In the brilliant sun they'd become giant crystal windchimes in the morning breeze. We walked from our cabin to the main lodge for breakfast through a blown glass village, boots crunching into the crisp snow. Our breath came out in huge dragon-like puffs.

I watched my breath for a while.

"Sandy, is it true that at the North Pole your breath turns solid when you talk and falls to the ground as bits of ice?" Sandy was a compulsive reader of footnotes and cereal boxes. I figured he might have run across this one.

"I never heard that."

I persisted. The idea of words freezing in mid-air appealed to my sense of whimsy and I wasn't ready to let the subject go.

"But wouldn't it be funny if it *did*? I mean, if the words we said came out of our mouths in different shapes so we could read what we were saying to each other like cartoons?"

Sandy wasn't willing to be dragged into Whimsyland before breakfast.

"A cup of coffee ought to fix you up," he said.

It frustrated me that Sandy wasn't a talker. Trying to get him to talk about ideas was like throwing a ball to a dog who just stands there and lets it drop in front of his paws.

But I still kept trying to get him to play.

"What do you think it is that actually cures people in psychotherapy?" I asked him the minute we got our ski jackets off and got settled into our booth in the lodge dining room. "Is it a function of the relationship? Is it simply the question of the patient feeling somebody cares? Is it insight? What do you think?"

"Beats me," Sandy said.

Usually the best way to get Sandy to talk was to ask for advice. When we'd ordered breakfast and had a first steaming cup of coffee, I started again.

"I need advice on how to handle a patient at the hospital in the locked ward," I said. "Every time I walk through the dayroom she runs up to me and says, 'Are you my mother?' I never know what to say to her. What do you think I should say?"

Sandy's eyes flickered. He was amused.

"Are you her mother?"

"No, of course not."

"Then tell her the truth."

"The truth?"

"The truth."

I was dumbfounded when Sandy gave me an answer like that. As soon as he said it, it seemed obvious. But whenever I tried to come up with a solution to a problem I complicated it. I'd spin my wheels

12

looking for clever answers and informed answers; it would never occur to me to ask myself, "What's the truth?"

The trouble with the truth was, it was too simple. It was just there. It was rarely something you could talk about or discuss. Here I wanted to chat about something with Sandy and now that we discovered the truth, there was nothing left to say. What fun was that? Why was it I could discuss things with my friend Mindy at work for hours and I couldn't even string five minutes together with Sandy.

Once I decided to discuss *this* with Sandy:

"Isn't the chemistry of conversations fascinating?" I said to him one Sunday morning as we were strolling along the Charles River in Boston where we lived. "I mean, isn't it interesting how some people can talk and their conversations are synergistic—they just take off—and other people find they're stuck for things to say to each other? How do you explain that?"

Sandy shrugged. He wasn't interested in talking about the chemistry of conversations either.

However, when it came to the telephone Sandy and I were two peas in a pod. You'd have thought being a talker I'd like the phone, but we both hated it.

Whenever it rang we'd look at each other and make a face.

Sometimes Sandy would say, "Let it ring."

"It's okay with me," I'd say. "You're the doctor."

"If it's a real emergency," he'd say, "they'll call a real doctor."

Actually, there was a part of me that agreed with Sandy about the virtues of not talking. Coming from a family of writers, I learned early to be on guard against the temptation to talk away ideas so by the time you sat down to write, the creative energy was dissipated.

My stepfather was guilty of this a lot.

"I've got a peach of an article idea, Bonnie," he'd announce to my mother at dinner.

My mother, herself a writer, would listen patiently—but only for a while. Then she'd interrupt:

"'Don't get it right, get it written,' Walt," she'd say and wink at him. It was a favorite family quote.

My stepfather would give her a sheepish grin and change the subject, "Anyone for some more salad?"

And the very next day, having awakened with the best of intentions to "get it written," Walt started his endless string of painful procrastinations—anything to avoid getting down to work.

13

He'd retired early from the publishing house he worked for just to write. Now both he and my mother were working at home.

While my mother wrote, Walt would putter around. By mid-morning he'd slip a little vodka into his orange juice and he'd carry it around with him as he walked outside along the edges of the huge lawn, checking out the hedges and flowers—"estate walking again," my mother would say as she watched him from the window. Then she'd get back to work.

Sometimes he'd get to the typewriter by late afternoon and sometimes he wouldn't get to it at all. But either way, sooner or later he'd end up back in the kitchen and make himself a "real" drink (no orange juice). If anybody was around he'd make a little joke. "It must be five o'clock somewhere," he'd say with a laugh. Then he'd go out and sit on the back porch with his drink and stare up the hill.

Tomorrow, at least, held the promise of being a good writing day.

The Sunday Sandy and I got back from Vermont, we got a phone call. For some reason Sandy played against type and answered it. It was his mother.

Hedy jumped right in. No hello, no how-are-you, no how-was-the-honeymoon—no nothing. Just, "Sanford, you have no idea what your damn sister said to us at brunch at Toots Shors this morning."

"I'll bite. What did she say?"

"She said—now listen to this—she said that when we lived in Bronxville your father used to hit her around."

"He did hit her around. I remember."

"That's not the point, Sanford. She said it out *loud* at Toots Shors. Toots was standing right there. She'd had too much to drink, as usual. It was embarrassing."

"She's thirty-three years old. You don't have to buy her breakfast."

"But she's our daughter."

"Then buy her breakfast and enjoy the abuse in good health," he said.

"That's not very sympathetic, Sanford!"

Sandy didn't provoke. He said nothing.

"Do you think she's an alcoholic?"

"Probably."

"Sanford, do you know what you're saying?"

And so it went, round and round.

I loved it. I loved it when Faye's drinking problem escalated into a crisis. It fed my thirst for drama—a thirst Sandy didn't share. He tolerated it; I needed it.

14

Late that night the Great Faye herself phoned just to tell Sandy to go fuck himself.

"Is this Sandy?"

"Yes, it is."

"You can go fuck yourself." Slam.

Sandy shrugged, hung up, and got back into bed.

I, on the other hand, was wide awake and energized. I wanted more than anything to talk.

"Why does Faye drink? What makes a person drink like that? Do you think she's *really* an alcoholic? (I loved the drama of that word.) Is it a symptom of something going on down deep inside? What happened to her when she was little to make her drink? Do you think maybe it was being hit around?"

"She always *was* a pain in the ass," Sandy said and rolled over and went back to sleep.

I was too hyped up to sleep.

I went into the kitchen and poured a jigger of Scotch into a glass of milk and drank it down.

After a blissfully short time, it did the trick.

# – 3 –

# PURPLE COWS

*I never saw a purple cow.*
*I never hope to see one.*
*But I can tell you anyhow,*
*I'd rather see than be one.*
                    *—Ogden Nash*

Mindy had pulled into the Boston State Hospital parking lot ahead of me and waited by her car while I parked.

It was my first day back to work after the honeymoon.

"Sadie, Sadie, Married Lady!" she said, grinning at me from behind another new pair of eyeglass frames. Finding the perfect pair was her obsession.

She gave me a hug and together we walked across the lawn to the administration building and down the outside staircase into the gloomy basement where the psychology department was located.

Psychology was at one end of a long, tan-tiled corridor and at the other end were two departments we refused to take seriously—social service and art therapy. We were snobs. We didn't mind relating "upwards" with analysts and psychiatrists, but avoided relating "downwards" with do-gooders and basket-weavers.

At the time Boston State Hospital, a mental institution, was home to some three thousand patients. They lived in old brick buildings on grounds which spread for many acres on both sides of busy Morton Street, dividing the "acute" side from the "chronic" side. The patients on the acute side were short-term and would probably go home again. Most of the patients on the chronic side were there for life.

Technically the hospital was in the Mattapan district of Boston. If you went nuts you got "sent to Mattapan."

Mindy was my best friend, which was thanks to her efforts more than mine. I was lazy about friendships, but if somebody I liked was willing to do most of the work, I'd go along. Now I was glad I had. We enjoyed each other. We made each other laugh.

"Some new psychiatric residents are here," Mindy said.

That wasn't good news. Whenever new psychiatrists arrived it meant more work for us. Most of them, at least at first, were unnerved working in a loony bin. They didn't trust themselves to diagnose anybody. So they referred patients to Psychology for testing so we could back them up: "Is this patient schizophrenic? Psychotic? Or what?"

Mindy and I had both been hired fresh out of graduate school. But she was better prepared to deal with crazies than I was. Her father was a psychiatrist who treated schizophrenics in his house so Mindy was used to patients hallucinating at the dinner table or sitting in her father's lap to "regress" for a spell. For her, Boston State was just like home.

But I was uncomfortable. My frame of reference was those "dentists" our family visited in Manhattan. So I distanced myself from patients. Patients were "them." Patients were "purple cows" I'd rather see than be. They weren't *me*.

"You know who is back?" Mindy said as we entered the big main office. "Dr. Green. You should see him. He's gorgeous."

"Dr. Green is gorgeous?"

"Wait'll you see. He got his nose fixed; he lost weight. You wouldn't recognize him."

Dr. Green was one of last year's new hot-shot psychiatric residents. He was overweight, had a big nose, and came on strong. One day he made a patient cross, so the patient "acted out" and bopped Dr. Green right on his big nose and broke it.

Dr. Green took a leave of absence to recover from his trauma leaving the other residents shaking in their penny loafers. Suddenly there was a new flurry of psychological testing requests: "What are the chances of this patient acting out?"

"If you ask me," Mindy said, "I think that patient did Dr. Green a favor!"

After the other staff members had welcomed me back, I went down the hall to my office and opened the door. The room was a small, cold cubicle with a high ceiling, buff-colored tile walls and a polished cement floor. It was like being inside a dirty icebox. Up near the ceiling a sliver of a window had bars on it. Whether the bars were to keep people from getting out—or getting in—wasn't clear to me.

A philodendron I'd left on the window ledge was dead. I never was good with plants. Out it went in the wastebasket. Once I left a dead plant like this hanging around and a patient I was supposed to test refused to work with me. He figured if I was a plant-killer, he could be next.

Aside from plants, I'm a nester. I even move motel furniture around. So I did what I could to make this dungeon cheerful—scatter rug, curtains, desk lamp, posters. Anything to warm up the place.

I did a little dusting and then I set off upstairs to the locked ward to see one of my caseload of individual psychotherapy patients—people I saw three times a week. I made sure to take my big bunch of noisy keys with me. Since the staff didn't get to wear little white coats, having official-looking keys was the only way you could tell who was who.

Anetta, my patient, was crazy. Most patients in mental hospitals aren't—at least they don't make the hairs on the back of your neck stand up—but Anetta was schizophrenic and, according to Mindy, she'd gone into a catatonic state while I'd been away.

"Probably a reaction to your going off and getting married," Mindy said. "I'm surprised *I* didn't have a reaction like that."

I found Anetta lying on her bed in her room, lanky arms rigidly at her sides, small, brown eyes riveted to the overhead bulb, jaw stuck open.

One of the new psychiatric residents was in the room when I got there. And sitting on the edge of Anetta's bed was an overweight woman with graying black hair and a black dress. I assumed she was Anetta's mother.

I was angry. I didn't want to meet Mother. If there was one thing that graduate school had taught me to *avoid* it was relatives. Social workers dealt with relatives.

Besides, I was laboring under an assumption that Anetta's craziness was her mother's fault.

So here I was, looking right into the eyes of the enemy: Mama!

I didn't know what to do.

The new psychiatric resident and the mother, however, didn't know that I didn't know what to do. They were both looking at me helplessly. Wasn't I Anetta's regular therapist? Wasn't I going to say something that would snap Anetta out of this catatonic nonsense and back to reality where they could all have a crack at her again?

If only this were the movies!

In movies therapists always know what to say. They know exactly what will work, how to dig right in there and unstick that repressed childhood trauma that's holding everything else up. They can ask just the right question at just the right moment to make catatonics like Anetta talk again.

But all I could think of to say was, "Hi."

No response.

"I was away getting married, Anetta. Do you remember?"

No response.

"Now I'm back. And I won't leave you again for a long, long time."

No response.

Finally Anetta's mother could stand it no longer. She threw herself onto her child and began to rock her stiffened body back and forth. "What makes her be like that?!" she wailed. "I don't understand it! What makes her *be* like that?"

Despite my efforts to tune the woman out, she got to me. I felt tears well up in my eyes. I, too, felt so terribly helpless. I fought the tears and felt embarrassed at what was happening to me. After all, I was a therapist and I wasn't supposed to let my buttons get pushed. I'd been trained to be a "blank screen"—so whatever emotions the patients *thought* they saw on my face was really a projection of their own emotions.

Glancing guiltily at Anetta, I reached for a box of kleenex and handed it to the weeping woman. She sat up and took it gratefully, wiping her eyes.

"I'm so embarrassed to cry like this," she said.

"It's okay," I said. I leaned down and put my hand on her shoulder to comfort her and to my horror she grabbed my hand in both of hers, brought it to her wet cheek—and wept some more.

During the entire scene, the psychiatric resident hung back as though witnessing something distasteful.

When I could pull myself away, I did. I made excuses about having to go and I fled from the room, the psychiatric resident hot on my heels.

20

"What do you think about the secondary-gain aspect of all this?" he asked as we sailed through the dayroom towards freedom. "I mean, isn't Anna—"

"—Anetta."

"—Anetta benefitting in some way from all this attention-getting behavior? Wouldn't you agree it's a passive-aggressive act to go catatonic on us?"

It sounded good to me. He was talking my kind of language.

But was it the truth? Why would somebody lie on a bed like a stick for weeks on end if they really had a choice?

"What do you think I should tell the mother?" the resident asked next.

It made me uncomfortable to have a psychiatrist asking *me* questions. He was relating downward. But I figured that was because he was new and still wet behind the ears. He'd learn.

"Maybe you should tell her not to visit Anetta so much. I think it upsets them both."

"Good idea!" he said. He seemed relieved. I don't think he liked relatives any more than I did. He peeled off and headed back to Anetta's room.

I felt relieved, too. The weeping woman would be out of the picture. But on a deeper level, just beyond my reach in that Cave of Truths we all seem to have down inside, I was bothered. I knew I was trying hard to push something away that I should have been nurturing and making an important part of my work. It took me a long, long time to figure that one out. It was love.

Back in the safety of my little office, I decided to tackle an easier patient: JoLynn.

I picked up the phone, called the B-Building, and asked JoLynn's ward doctor to have an attendant bring her over to see me.

When the attendant arrived with JoLynn, he couldn't wait to tell me the news: "She did it again!" He pointed to JoLynn's freshly bandaged wrists. "On her weekend pass she did it. Show her, JoLynn."

JoLynn nonchalantly held up her arms. "Exhibit A," she said.

"We'll talk about it," I said. I told the attendant to come back for her in an hour and I shut my office door.

JoLynn slunk down in the wooden chair across the desk from me (desks made great barriers). She was wearing a long-sleeved white nylon sweater. The plunging V-neck showed off a generous bosom. She was slender, pretty, had dark hair and blue eyes and teeth that were slightly, attractively bucked.

21

She plucked at the threads of her wrist bandages. She wouldn't look at me. I made a mental note that she was "avoiding eye contact." Once a week I had to discuss each of my cases with my psychiatric supervisor and I'd learned that this was one of the phrases therapists can use to make themselves look good and the patient look not so good. To say that patients "avoid eye contact" suggests they're hiding something, whereas simply stating "the patient looked down a lot" might indicate mere shyness. "The patient denies..." was another handy phrase. Hiding something again, maybe an unconscious impulse, which certainly hinted at something more significant than "the patient said 'No' when I asked her if she had hostility towards her mother."

You could expect patients to lie and deny. That's why they were patients. They didn't know themselves. That's why they needed our help.

"What happened this time?" I asked JoLynn.

"Same as last. I don't remember."

I gave a small laugh. "You don't remember cutting your wrists?"

"No."

"How's *that*?"

"I'd had beer."

"Because something was bothering you?"

"No, why should it?"

"You weren't bothered because I went off and got married?"

JoLynn's mother had died when JoLynn was nine, so it was a safe bet to interpret that being deserted by a mother figure (like me, for example—even though I was only a few years older) was an important and traumatic theme in her life.

When I said that, JoLynn looked me right in the eye ("making eye contact") and said: "To tell you the truth, I didn't even remember you were getting married, so I wouldn't make a federal case out of it."

I felt myself flush. I never knew what to say when a patient disagreed with one of my psychological interpretations. Do you argue with them about it? ("Yes, you do!" "No, I don't!") I would never have dared question one of my own therapist's interpretations. I always figured they knew more about me than I did.

"Then what did you cut your wrists for?" I said, recovering by going on the attack.

"I already told you—I don't know."

"What happened just before you did it?"

"I drank the beer. My dad took my kids to the store and I drank beer."

22

"But what happened to upset you to make you drink beer? *That's* what's important."

"Nothing. I just drank it."

I was getting exasperated with this round-robin. "JoLynn, people don't drink too much beer for no reason and cut their wrists for no reason."

She hesitated for a second and "avoided eye contact" again. "They do if they're alcoholic," she said, almost inaudibly.

That one threw me.

"Where did you hear that?"

"At the Alcoholics Anonymous meeting. Last night the nurse brought me over to the AA meeting they have upstairs in the auditorium. She goes."

"And they told you that?" This was getting to be a bit much.

"They don't tell you. You just figure it out."

"And that's what you figured out?—that you're alcoholic!" I said sarcastically.

She nodded. "You don't think I am?"

"Of course not. You're only twenty-three years old."

She looked genuinely disappointed, which surprised me. I thought she'd be pleased.

Before I left to go home that night I made a call to JoLynn's ward doctor (whose wishes, I knew, would take precedence over the whim of some nurse) and recommended that he *not* give JoLynn another pass for another AA meeting. I explained that I was working with her in therapy on getting to the root of her drinking problem—which of course was painful for her—so it wasn't surprising that she wanted to use this AA thing to avoid treatment. However, it couldn't go on. I said I was sure he'd understand.

He did. Perfectly.

JoLynn's next request for an AA pass was denied.

# – 4 –

# WHAT LION?

*Denial: a defense mechanism; the refusal to acknowledge
a source of distress. For example, a man being chased by
a lion says, "What lion?"*
     —The Psychodynamic Perspective

All my life I've had a lot of energy. The only way I ever knew it was
a lot, or more than normal, was that other people kept telling me it
was a lot. "Where do you get your energy?" they'd say.

Once in our Manhattan duplex on East 75th Street, I broadjumped
over the couch, missed, and put my teeth through my lower lip. I still
have the scar.

Years earlier when I was only four or five, my mother discovered
that sugar made me worse. If I had a coke before bedtime I'd be up
half the night. Same thing with chocolate: "It makes her drunk, I
swear." (When I saw Lee Remick munching chocolate in *Days of
Wine and Roses*, I identified!)

As an adult, sugar made my head spin with ideas and I'd want to
talk. When Sandy proved to be part Trappist monk, I had to find new
ways of dealing with excess piss and vinegar.

Which I did.

A martini before dinner tamed my brain. Now, instead of my thoughts
racing out there three feet ahead of my body, thanks to martinis they
stayed put in my skull. I no longer had to chase down every idea. I
could just sit down and rest.

Sandy didn't know what caused it, I'm sure, but I think at first he
was relieved that I didn't overwhelm him when he got home.

But then there was the flip side.

25

"You used to get up and greet me at the door after work," he said a bit sadly one night. "Is the honeymoon over?"

My stomach sank. I knew what he said was true—and I knew it had something to do with gin. Gin was somehow running interference in my marriage, making me lazy. But for reasons which at the time eluded me, I didn't want Sandy to know gin had anything to do with it. Just as I didn't want him to know that gin had anything to do with my forgetting little things, like did I listen to the eleven o'clock news last night or not?

I put the spotlight of blame on myself instead.

"There's a lot of stuff going on at work," I said. "By the time I get home, I'm too bushed to move."

The lie came rolling trippingly off my tongue.

Why, I wondered, had I just lied to cover up for gin?

Sandy seemed to be thriving at work. He was still being John Wayne out there, ahead of the pack, scouting out new ways of doing shrink work when his colleagues were happy being Freudian disciples.

It all made me uneasy. I'd gone through college and graduate school impatient to get to the important stuff—Sigmund Freud and psychoanalytic theory. I'd barely paid attention to anything else. It wasn't "relevant." Freud to me was clearly The Answer. Yet here was Sandy, rocking boats, threatening to throw Freud overboard. It shook me up. Why was he doing this? Why couldn't he stick to what was already working just fine?

Sandy kept trying new techniques, his current favorite being "push the patient in the direction of the symptom." If a patient complained of overeating, smoking or drinking too much, instead of telling him or her to stop, Sandy would "prescribe the symptom"—ask the patient to do *more*: eat more, smoke more, drink more. If a patient was impotent or couldn't sleep, Sandy would forbid him to make love or try to sleep, telling him to wax the kitchen floor instead—twice if necessary.

The theory behind all this was that all patients rebel. Sooner or later patients would come into Sandy's office and admit, sheepishly, that they'd disobeyed orders: they'd stopped overeating, stopped smoking or drinking or they'd made love or slept.

Problem solved.

"That's manipulation!" I said, even though I was impressed that he could pull off a stunt like this.

"That's bad?"

"Yeah, it's a bad word."

Sandy shrugged. "Maybe, but it works. If the patients are getting what they came for, so what?"

"I'm not comfortable with that."

"You'd rather they *didn't* get what they came for if it means doing a manipulation?"

I thought about that for a minute.

"Yes."

One day Mindy showed me an article about psychotherapy in the *Saturday Evening Post*. It suggested that psychotherapy, statistically, is no more effective than no therapy at all.

Those were fighting words!

I was furious.

I wrote my first angry letter to a magazine, insisting that therapy *does too* work—and I gave case histories to prove it.

But somewhere inside me in the Cave of Truths that remained so shadowy and out of reach, I knew better. In spite of all the years I'd spent in analysis and therapy (I was still in therapy), I knew I hadn't changed. And I knew that I hadn't changed anybody else. People who got better did it themselves, as though "struck better" by a whim of fate, not by me.

When I discussed the ones who got "cured" with my supervisor, he always gave me the credit: "Good job of therapy, Sylvia."

Getting the credit made me feel like an angel and I still loved feeling like an angel, so I accepted it.

But it wasn't really satisfying.

It didn't answer my deepest questions, like why do some people change and some don't.

The truth about healing was a mystery.

I walked into work one morning and Mindy was waiting for me.

"Guess who we got in over the weekend?"

She was excited.

"Who?"

"Nanci Dean!"

"You're kidding."

"No, really. Nanci Dean."

Nanci Dean had been making headlines in the Boston papers all week for pushing her two children, ages one and three, out of a Boston hotel room window and killing them. Now she was here at Boston State for observation to determine if she was sane enough to stand trial. The assumption, of course, was that she wasn't. Anybody who'd do a thing like that *had* to be crazy.

"And guess who's been assigned to do the testing? You!"

"Why me?" My first thought was, it's a responsibility—and I don't want it.

"You're next on the list and Fred says we can't handle her differently even if she is a celebrity. You're so lucky! I'd give anything to test her—they're all talking about her upstairs."

How we loved notorious patients ("Jack the Ripper was my patient, you know"), people like Nanci Dean or the man who'd staked out at the top of a flagpole for four days threatening to shoot anybody who tried to get him down. He'd ended up with us.

"I'll do five of your other testing referrals if you'll let me do Nanci Dean," Mindy said.

By now I was getting caught up in the excitement. I shook my head. "Uh-uh. It'll be something I can tell my grandchildren."

Mindy got one of her mischievous looks on her face: "You mean when they're about age one and age three?"

To my astonishment, Nanci Dean didn't test crazy.

How was that possible? How could she *not* be?

I spent over an hour talking to her before I administered any tests. She was charming, pretty, and proved to have a wry sense of humor and a literary way of describing things.

"Do you write?" I finally asked her.

She laughed. It had an edge of bitterness to it. "Who has time! Since my husband split, I've had to live with my parents—we don't get along—and work two jobs to support the kids. Why?"

"Just that you have a writer's way of describing things, that's all."

"Looks like now I may have all the time in the world to write."

Nanci Dean knew right from wrong and knew what she'd done was wrong and was appropriately remorseful: "It will haunt me for the rest of my life."

"Where did her madness disappear to!" I wailed to Sandy. "She *has* to be nuts! Where *is* it! I must have given the Rorschach wrong. Maybe I should fudge the results. Should I fudge the results?"

I looked at Sandy. He didn't answer—he just waited.

"I know, don't say it: Tell the truth. Right?"

"That's one way you could go," Sandy said.

"But what *is* the truth? How does a person find out what that is?"

Sandy pointed to his chest. "Check in here," he said.

"What does that mean?"

He shrugged and went back to his reading.

During the week or so before I had to go to court with my not-crazy psychological report on Nanci Dean, I kept mulling over our conversation in my mind, especially some of Nanci's answers to questions about the details of that fateful night when she'd pushed her kids out onto Copley Square.

"I just don't remember it. I blanked out," was her answer.

My automatic assumption here was that this "blanked out" story was something her lawyer told her to say to cover herself so I didn't pursue it. That was between them. Nor did I connect it with stories she'd told me earlier about life at home with her parents and how she'd drink and sometimes "blank out."

"Some of my evenings were like Swiss cheese," she laughed. "They had holes in them!"

I needn't have worried about being the only one to find Nanci Dean sane. It was amazing how many people in that hospital had found an excuse to interview her and show up in court to tell all about it.

The consensus was that Nanci Dean, while not crazy *now*, most likely *had* been crazy at the time she committed the crime—and the act itself had snapped her out of it.

"Now what that tells us," Sandy said rather dryly later on, "is that murder *heals*."

Nor was I the only one to assume that Nanci's lawyer was behind her oft-repeated statement that she couldn't remember the details of that night because she had "blanked out."

Being lawyer-inspired, it was dealt with as insignificant.

There were even a few psychiatrists who ventured to put forth another theory. Nanci Dean, they said, was a typical hysteric personality and blanking out was an hysteric's way of handling unpleasantness—a convenient "forgetting" of a traumatic event.

The conclusion was this: Since Nanci Dean had to have been (not *was* but *had* to have been) crazy at the time of the murder, she should remain hospitalized now and be re-evaluated at some later date to see then if she was sane enough to stand trial.

"Proving," Sandy went on to say, "that down is up and black is white."

Not once during the entire episode had Nanci Dean's drinking been mentioned.

And I was one of the people who never mentioned it.

# – 5 –

# SANFORD

*Sanford (from Alexander): powerful ruler.*
—*Definition in* Name Your Baby

Some women say there are only two kinds of men: the ones who are exciting and mean to you—and the ones who are boring and love you. Up until the time I met Sandy, I'd seen only one kind of man—the kind that falls apart.

My real father, Boo (the name stuck after he once jumped out at me and made something of an impression), fell apart after a rather magical decade of being the darling of East Coast literary circles, triggered by the publication of his readable history of the American Revolution when he was only eighteen. This was followed by another history, a couple of novels and, just after I was born, an interview with Gertrude Stein which appeared in a book on the creative process. In it Gertrude and he take a moment out to discuss "darling baby Sylvia."

When I was three and Boo figured I was old enough to meet the Connecticut literati, he took me along for the ride. And at one such outing, I'm told, I got to sit on Theodore Dreiser's knee.

I'm afraid I don't remember those folks too well, but what I *do* remember was how many of them couldn't resist quoting "Ah, who is Sylvia and what is she that all the swains adore her!" the minute my father introduced them to me.

Boo had his fall-apart when I was four. His psychiatrist decided to hospitalize him in Westport. At first Boo refused until the doctor told him it was the very same hospital where Zelda Fitzgerald had spent time.

31

That's when Boo agreed to go.

Using an old car with a rumble seat that was either borrowed or belonged to the psychiatrist, we all drove off to the mental hospital one humid, overcast summer Sunday afternoon. The psychiatrist was up in front with my mother and Boo was back in the rumble seat with me.

Somewhere on a lonely stretch of country road ribboning through open fields, Boo had one of his increasingly frequent seizures. He gazed up at the blackening sky, moaned, and holding tightly onto his briefcase which contained his latest manuscript (he intended to finish it in the sanitarium), he keeled over into my lap.

I shrieked bloody murder.

I tried to push him back into a sitting position but he was way too heavy for me. Finally, I wiggled out from under him and stood up so I could pound on the car's rear window.

The psychiatrist pulled over to the side of the road, jumped out, and came rushing to our rescue.

When the excitement was all over I was let down.

That's when I first discovered my thirst for drama.

My stepfather Walt's fall-apart happened years later when I was in junior high school. Walt didn't go to a sanitarium. He crumbled right there in the comfort of his own home, surrounded by his impressive collection of books on mental health.

He lay on the couch in his darkened office and no one except my mother was allowed through the door. It was now the second time in her life a man had passed on the torch of responsibility to her and she carried on like a little soldier.

From her, I think, came so many of my own little soldier "I'll do it myself, thank you" traits.

She held the household world together so the protector and provider could disintegrate in peace.

She refused to rise to the bait when I pushed at her to discuss his case. She never criticized anyone and she wasn't about to start now. When a doctor came (I don't know what kind) and asked how much Walt had been drinking, I remember she minimized it with "cocktails at five o'clock before dinner."

No more was said.

After about three weeks, Walt began to pull out of it. He appeared now at the dinner table, looking pale from being in the dark for so long, but as always kind and attentive to my sister Justine and to me. Just as though nothing had happened.

Even my first husband, Lucas, turned out to be a collapser. He'd survived Hitler in Vienna as a young music student; he'd survived the Blitz in London where he'd gone to escape from Austria (he was half-Jewish) and continue his studies; he'd survived an ocean voyage across the torpedo infested Atlantic Ocean; he'd survived three weeks at Ellis Island; he survived the indignity of having to play in Hungarian restaurants in New York. But when his life got stable and respectable again (he'd been hired by a chamber music group) he went wacky. After we'd been married a year or so, he became obsessed that somebody was out to hurt his hands.

When he made the two of us leave a family restaurant one night because there were tough-looking characters about, I knew we were in trouble. That, plus the fact that he was unrelentingly mean.

I made sure that both Lucas *and* his hands were under the care of a psychiatrist before I left him.

But Sandy was different. Sandy was solid. Sandy was too smart to cave in.

And in spite of the fact that I couldn't get more than twenty-five words or less out of him in one sitting, we were happy.

We flowed along together like two bits of balsa wood bobbing downstream. It was effortless. It was easy. In fact, when people said you have to *work* at marriage, I didn't understand what they meant.

"Are we *working* at this relationship?" I asked Sandy one night.

"Should we be?"

"That's what people say."

"They don't mean us."

That answer was good enough. In fact, that answer was good enough for a lot of things.

It was February and our first anniversary. Sandy made a reservation at Joseph's and I left work early to have time to dress up. Before I sat down at my dressing table to put on my make-up, I made myself my "get-dressed" martini—the martini *before* the martinis I'd order after we got to Joseph's. It was a new addition to my routine. "Why don't you wait until we get there?" Sandy asked innocently. "Better to do it now. I could get hit by a Mack truck on the way," I answered.

When Sandy got home from his day in Cambridge (he worked in a student health service part-time) and walked into the bedroom, I knew something was wrong.

"What *is* it?"

"One of my patients just shot his head off," he said matter-of-factly.

"Oh, God!"

I studied him to see if I could get a reading on how he was taking it. I couldn't. Besides, I was starting to get hung up on what he'd just said.

"Did you say he shot his head *off*? Like right off his neck? Or did you mean he shot himself *in* the head? Which?"

"*In* the head," Sandy said, irritated for a second.

"In your office?"

"No, in his mother's backyard."

"He lived at home?"

Sylvia, shut up! I told myself. Why are you asking questions?

"No, he lived at Harvard. He just went home to shoot his head off."

I sat there waiting for Sandy to say more while dozens of even more trivial questions popped into my head. I had to fight to keep from asking them.

"Is that *it*?" I finally said.

Sandy nodded.

"You mean we're still going out to dinner?"

"Staying home won't change anything," he said. .

I had no answer for that one. Still, it seemed strange.

"Are you sure?"

"I'll go get the car," he said.

It was bitter cold. The wind whipped across the Charles River. I don't like wind. Wind feels like an attack and I want to push back.

It felt good to get into the car.

"How did you find out about it?" I asked once we were on our way. I couldn't resist another question.

"His mother called me. She said she hoped I could learn enough from this experience so I could see it coming next time."

"She said that?" I was horrified. How come Sandy wasn't even horrified? He looked so damn calm yet I was sure the mother's words must have lacerated him. "That goddamned bitch!" I said.

I was shocked at myself; after all, the poor woman had just lost a son. But damn, what a low blow—to which Sandy seemed oblivious.

Across from Joseph's, Sandy pulled the car over to the curb. At first I thought he was preparing to make a U-turn for the valet parking attendant, who was standing out front, heavy coat on, hopping up and down to keep warm.

34

Instead, Sandy stopped the car and turned off the motor. Then he put both arms up on the steering wheel, leaned over and rested his forehead on them.

He was silent and I sat there, holding my breath. What was happening?

"I don't feel well," Sandy finally said. "Let's go home."

Back in the apartment, Sandy sat almost cowering at one end of the long, stark, charcoal gray Dux couch. I sat tentatively at the other end, waiting.

"I didn't see it coming!"

The suddenness of his outcry and the pain in his voice startled me.

"I had no idea he was suicidal! None! I *missed* it!"

I didn't know what to do, how to behave, what to say. Sandy was always so unruffled, so sure; he'd never seemed helpless before.

I sat perched there, feeling stiff and awkward, fighting an impulse within me to go to him and hold him.

Finally, even though I was fearful that it was the wrong thing to do and Sandy would be irritated—I even pictured him swinging out at me—I got up and then gingerly I sat down next to him, put my arms around him and held onto him tightly.

Touching him seemed to take the keystone out of his self-control. All at once he collapsed into my arms and wept.

My heart began to pound. I felt a surge of joy. Finally, finally, he had let me in.

And then another feeling, buried even deeper inside of me, surfaced: panic.

Was Sandy just another man who would fall apart after all?

# – 6 –

# REPRIEVE

*Insight doesn't cure anybody. Knowledge of the law of gravity doesn't help if you're falling from the fifth floor.*
—*Attributed to Sigmund Freud*

*Understanding is the booby prize.*
—*Werner Erhard*

From that anniversary evening on, Sandy sealed over and handled the suicide of his patient with clinical detachment. He played psychiatrist to himself. He'd remark on his mental condition as though discussing the case history of someone else.

"I'm still depressed," he'd say. "I'm not sleeping well. My energy level is down. And I've developed a fear of my work. I think everybody wants to commit suicide. Anytime someone mentions feeling bad I want to hospitalize him."

He read articles in psychiatric journals about coping with suicidal patients. He read books on loss, on guilt.

He understood it all.

And he stayed depressed.

There seemed to be no one he talked to. I hadn't noticed until now that he had no friends. He never got a personal phone call—except, of course, from his mother or Faye.

"Maybe you should see a psychiatrist," I suggested.

Sandy gave me one of his wry little smiles. "I don't believe in psychiatrists."

He turned down three referrals in a row to his private practice. "I

37

don't want to see them," he said. "They're too depressed. I referred them to somebody else."

Instead of building up his practice, he took on more administrative duties at the student health service and accepted a consultant spot at a small private hospital. He managed to tie up a lot of hours supervising other psychiatrists.

All of which kept him from dealing directly with patients himself.

Sandy had been bucked off and was refusing to get back up on the horse.

We began to spend our evenings in different rooms. Sandy stayed in the living room and I stayed in the bedroom. We'd watch the same TV show on different sets. He'd munch on goodies and I'd sip on gin. When I had something to say to him I had to raise my voice or wave my hand in front of his face to get his attention; he was that lost inside himself.

For his birthday I bought him a telescope so he could gaze up at the universe and hopefully get a little perspective on things.

It didn't work. He used it to look into the windows of the Charter House Motel across the Charles River.

"The only difference between you and a Peeping Tom is the distance you are from your subject!" I snapped at him one evening.

Things were beginning to get a little nasty. We made love less and less. And sometimes after we'd retreated into our separate cells, I'd get a whiff of a feeling of a third presence hovering over our lives: There was Sandy. There was me. And there was this martini I'd sneaked into the bedroom, sitting on the bedside table next to me. Why did I feel guilty about that, as though I'd taken on a lover?

Sandy got a reprieve from his depression.

What did it was my pregnancy.

Maybe this was because pregnancy is about giving life—just what Sandy needed after the suicide had made him feel like a destroyer.

He went on a diet. He did Air Force exercises in the living room. He bought us tickets to things. "I'm making an effort to connect us to the outside world," he explained. "We've been too isolated." He even cut back on the smoking and the telescope.

On my end, I stopped drinking gin. It happened automatically. The pregnancy made me too queasy to drink.

Without gin, my brain-tamer, I couldn't sleep. I was keyed up.

Finally my gynecologist prescribed a pill called Doriden.

What a pill!

Doriden was like getting hit with a merry-go-round. It made me dizzy and giddy and giggly and happy and, above all, talkative again!

Now at night I'd go on talking jags that lasted an hour after the light was out. If my mother thought chocolates before bedtime made me high, she should have seen me now.

Sandy usually fell asleep while I was still in mid-sentence.

Poor Sandy!

Ah, pills. Doriden was only the beginning.

For years, because Sandy was a physician, pills in all colors rained down upon us every day, falling through the mail slot of our apartment and landing on the foyer floor. Drug companies sent them, hoping Sandy would prescribe them for his patients. Valium, Dexedrine, Ritalin, Nembutal, Seconal, uppers, downers, sideway-ers, pink ones, green ones, blue ones, orange ones, round ones, heart-shaped ones, oval ones.

"Pretty!" our daughter Emily exclaimed when she was old enough to crawl over to the front door where the pill samples landed.

*Pretty*, in fact, was her very first word!

"No, Emily, phoofy!" I'd say. "Let Mommy have those!"

"PRETTY!" she'd protest as I snatched them away.

"Yes, honey, I know. *Very* pretty."

And they were. Pretty enough to eat.

What mail we didn't eat, we collected in a box and donated to the Massachusetts General Hospital.

Usually what we held back were Dexedrine (which Sandy was now taking and my mother liked, too), Ritalin (same type of thing), Nembutal (sleeping pill), Miltowns (already going out of style,) and of course, Valium.

Nothing excessive.

I figured going to sleep without "taking something" was a lost childhood art. Grown-ups needed something to relax.

But during the pregnancy I stuck to Doriden.

I *loved* Doriden.

To celebrate the diagnosis of pregnancy, Sandy and I spent a week at the Plaza Hotel.

We walked and window-shopped and made all our family visits, which was a chore. Sandy's parents both came from large broods. They practically made up their own home town. There were a couple of aunts I'd never met who'd been "put away," apparently quite bonkers. And of course, with great relish on my part, we got to hear all the latest gossip about Faye's drinking.

We felt closer than we had in a year. Sandy, slimmer now, looked marvelous and I looked like I was supposed to—healthy and fat. We took lots of pictures of each other (including pregnant tummy, now kicking) and spent three hours in FAO Schwartz playing with toys.

I'd never seen Sandy so loose.

Pregnancy became him.

For nostalgia's sake, Sandy took me to a cafeteria on 57th Street where he used to hang out when he was in medical school.

"You know what happened to me here once?" he said.

My God, he was actually initiating a conversation.

"What? What!?" I said, probably sounding overly eager but I was so excited he was talking.

Sandy went right on. "I came in here with a couple of my med school classmates, guys I really admired. We sat in that booth over there by the window. We were looking at the menu—and out of the corner of my eye I saw this bag lady on the sidewalk, trying to maneuver her shopping cart full of junk. Next thing I know, she's in here, going from table to table begging for money. I remember thinking, oh-oh—better have some change ready so we can get rid of her fast. I was reaching into my pocket when I heard this yell: 'Sandy! Sandy, is that you?!' Suddenly she's right over me and she's got her dirty fingers on my chin—God, what a stench—and she's squeezing it saying 'Oy, God, I don't believe it! Little Sandy! Don't you remember me? It's your Aunt Miriam!' By now the guys I was with were looking at me—"

"—in a new way I bet!" I was roaring with laughter.

"Definitely in a new way!"

"What did you do?"

"What could I do? I introduced them to her. And they all shook her fishy hand very politely like nothing was even out of line."

Now he was laughing: "That was my lesson in humility. Whenever I get into my Dr. God number, I think of that."

We left the restaurant and walked back out onto busy 57th Street again.

"Do you know what happened to *me* once, right about *here*?" I pointed down to the sidewalk. "I was here with Lucas when his chamber music group was playing Carnegie Hall. I got him to let me carry his violin. I *begged* him to let me carry his violin—all because I hoped maybe somebody passing us would think *I* was a violinist."

Suddenly I got tears in my eyes remembering how insignificant I felt during that marriage. Sandy caught it and put his arm around me and held me close. "That's kind of sad," he said.

Back in Boston in the dressing room of the Ecole de Ballet on Beacon Street (I took classes well into my sixth month) I told my fellow student, Corliss, all about the bag lady in New York who turned out to be Sandy's aunt. Corliss was a social worker and this immediately triggered another discussion in our running series of nature vs. nurture arguments. I was nurture; Corliss was nature. I was environment; Corliss was heredity.

"Sandy's aunt is probably schizophrenic," Corliss said, "something I'm convinced is biochemical. It's got nothing to do with not being loved enough or when she went on solid foods."

"Environment causes schizophrenia," I said with equal conviction.

"I know you *think* that, but you're wrong," she said.

As we went upstairs for ballet class, I wondered how somebody could just say "You're wrong" like that. What was I doing "relating downwards" to a social worker, anyway? What did they know about personality dynamics? Social workers were supposed to stick to practical things, like how to deal with landlords.

Still, I persisted even when we were doing pliés at the barre.

"Something must have been funny in the home for old Auntie Miriam to have turned into a bag lady," I said.

"Horseshit!"

Corliss floored me. I'd always wanted to be able to say "horseshit!" to somebody but never dared. But Corliss just said it right out.

"I've worked with lots of schizophrenics," she went on. "Some of them came from very happy homes. Now how do you explain that?"

"Maybe you just *missed* something. Maybe they weren't all that happy. Maybe a psychiatrist would have been able to see it."

Answer *that* one, Corliss Social-Worker!

Corliss didn't exactly smirk, but you could feel a smirk in the room. "One of these days you'll find out that psychiatrists go to the bathroom like anybody else."

We probably would have kept this going another few rounds if Monsieur Pierre himself, his flaming red hair sticking out in all directions, hadn't put a stop to it. He was angry that we were talking in class.

"Mademoiselle Sylvie! Mademoiselle Cor-leese! *Attention!* S'il vous plaît!" He pointed his stick at us accusingly and then tap-tapped with it on the floor to drive home his point. "Plié. PLIÉ! PLIÉ!"

41

We both pliéd.

When he'd moved on, Corliss leaned over, gave me a gentle pat on my bulging stomach and shot me one last zinger: "Things may not seem quite so simple to you, Sylvia, once you've had a kid."

# – 7 –

# EMILY

*No problem is so serious that we cannot successfully run away from it.*
—*Linus in* Peanuts

When I woke up with labor pains a week ahead of schedule, I was disappointed; I liked being pregnant. I wasn't ready to give it up yet. In the operating room of Boston Lying-In Hospital, I threw my arms around my stomach just to hang onto it a bit longer.

"That's not helping," a nurse said.

Another nurse and she took one arm each and held them down at my sides so the event could continue unhampered.

I was conscious. They held Emily so I could see her and then they placed her near me in a little plastic bed. I was happy for a moment—and then out of nowhere in the middle of a smile, I was hit with a chill of fear. "What's going on here?" I remember thinking. Suddenly I felt as though, in giving birth to this fragile little girl, I'd just done something unspeakably, primevally wrong.

But *what?*

A childhood scene I hadn't thought of in years came back to me. When I was five I'd "murdered" my doll after learning that my mother had just sent my nurse Mae packing. Now my mother had done this for a good reason. My father and Mae had been having an affair. But I was crushed. I adored Mae. We'd shared a room together off the kitchen. Now I'd never see her again. And she'd left without even saying goodbye.

43

When I heard the news I knew just what I was going to do. I walked into my bedroom, got the doll off my bed that my mother had bought me as a "Friday present" (she worked, and every Friday she came home with a surprise), took the doll into the kitchen, got a pair of scissors and in a very deliberate way I stabbed it and stabbed it and stabbed it. To this day I can still taste my fury as I performed this dirty deed. And as I did this I remember making a vow (the logic of which eludes me now) that when *I* had a child of my own, *this* is what I'd do to it!

Then I pulled the insides out, pulled the legs and arms off, wrapped it all up in a brown paper bag and threw it in the garbage under the kitchen sink.

When it was all over I knew I was a "child murderer" to the core.

And now I had a real child of my own!

I couldn't tell Sandy what had been happening in my soul. It was too strange. So I lay there in my hospital bed all during that first day of Emily's life, almost breathless from anxiety, and tried to behave like I was sane.

Sandy was so happy. His parents came up from New York. Mine came up from Connecticut. They made such a fuss—they were wonderful. So I held on.

And then, just as swiftly as the haunting had come, it went away.

Motherhood made me edgy—I felt restless and bored. I began to put pressures on myself to make better use of my time. I should be doing something constructive, accomplishing something. When I nursed Emily, I'd try to read *Time* magazine at the same time.

Emily fought breastfeeding as much as I did. She preferred a bottle. But when I called my gynecologist to tell him that Emily and I both wanted out, he threw me a curve: "You made a contract with your child to breast feed her for six months. If you choose to break that contract that's up to you. Is that what you want to do?"

I wasn't prepared for this. My heart began to pound. *What* contract? I didn't remember making any contract! My stomach knotted up—a clue to let me know I was angry. ("A knot in the gut is an unexpressed *No*," I learned later.) Only then I didn't acknowledge such things. Instead, I fled into guilt and shame, like a little girl being scolded over the big phone by "daddy." Oh, God! I said to myself. He's so right! I'm a terrible person! A doll-murderer!

So I didn't even try to defend myself or explain what had been going on. I just shut up.

"Well," the doctor was saying, "what's your decision?"

"I'll think about it," I said. I was shaking.

"You do that," he said.

That was the night I crossed some kind of dividing line. A switch in my head that had been in the *off* position was flipped *on*.

I made myself a huge drink.

Going down, it was warm. It hit the steel knot in my gut and immediately dissolved it. Nothing was left but oatmeal. I began to breathe again. The gynecologist's voice faded. After the first drink, the petty stuff of daily life began to come into perspective.

After the second drink, then a third, I didn't care if it was in perspective or not.

Gin works.

Sometimes as I was sliding into drunkenness, I used to think it would be a kick to put green dye in a martini and X-ray it as it coursed its way through the human body—watch it go through the bloodstream, through every vessel, artery, capillary, and vein—watch it sweep its way across the brain—watch it pulsate through the heart—boomboom! boomboom! boomboom!

In no time at all, I was waiting for a "decent" hour to begin to drink. The knot in my stomach would be insistent. It needed immediate oatmealing.

I'd walk into the kitchen and remember my stepfather's little jokes after he'd come in from his day of procrastinating and estate-walking—how he'd say, "Oh, well, it must be five o'clock somewhere!" as he made himself a drink.

Then I'd make myself a drink.

I was back to little lies—like the lies I told to cover up my loss of appetite: "I'm not hungry because I ate lunch late" or "I'm not hungry because I had a snack when I got home." Lies.

Sometimes I'd sit at the dinner table just for show and pick at food. Sometimes I'd sit and drink my dinner (and tell my lies) while Sandy ate his. And sometimes I'd serve Sandy dinner and then disappear into the bedroom with my "lover" gin and watch TV.

If I wanted a refill, I'd wait until I heard Sandy go into the bathroom and then I'd make a dash into the kitchen, grab some ice cubes, pour more gin over them (no time for the vermouth) and dash back as soon as I heard the toilet flush.

The blackouts began happening on a regular basis—though I didn't know that's what they were. I called it "falling asleep early."

One morning Sandy commented on a story on last night's eleven o'clock news. When he said it, I realized I didn't even remember last night's eleven o'clock news.

Of course, I couldn't let on that I didn't remember. Sandy might say, "Don't drink" and I couldn't have that happen, so I bluffed my way through.

Physically, Emily was beautiful. Her perfectly formed and proportioned little facial features made her look like a miniature grown-up instead of a baby. She had a full head of dark hair and my mother's cornflower blue eyes. One eye was almost imperceptibly askew—a feature I had once read is the sign of a spiritual being.

But Emily was "different."

That, too, was imperceptible at first, nothing I could put my finger on. It was more of a feeling I had about her. There was a "not-thereness" quality about her. She smiled and she played and she did all the physical things like sit, crawl, stand, and walk right on schedule—even early— but sometimes I'd look at her and find myself thinking, "She's a Martian."

Emily didn't relate to people so much as "trip out" on them, watch them like they were mobiles before her eyes, moving, speaking, but it wasn't personal. If their noises were loud, she got scared.

The older Emily got, the more uneasy I got that others would notice her strangeness. I anticipated judgments, blame. I'd put the doll-murderer memory back on the shelf, but on another level I was left with this sense that I had done something dreadful to Emily—that whatever was wrong was my fault.

It was painful.

We hired a nurse, Mrs. Owens—a stoic but sweet woman who was the widow of a compulsive gambler (he'd wiped them out and now she had to work). She was a real nurse, white uniform and all, and her being there meant I could go back to work three days a week at a new job, of all places, in a child guidance center.

Having a "title" again helped my frame of mind. I couldn't stand it if people thought I was "just a housewife." I'd have worked even if I didn't want to just to avoid that.

As soon as Emily was old enough, we sent her to a charming Catholic nursery school run by nuns in the Newton woods. I loved the serenity of the place.

But serenity or no serenity, it would be just a matter of time before I received the first of what would be a steady stream of inevitable phone calls from Emily's teachers.

Pretty soon it came.

"Emily seems to be in a dream world," Sister Irene said. "We're concerned. We try, but we can't reach her, can't even get her attention. Have you thought of having her *seen* by somebody?"

Interesting! I thought. Now nuns referred you to psychiatrists instead of to God.

"Maybe we should have her evaluated," I said to Sandy.

"Most winds blow themselves," Sandy said.

But this one didn't.

There were more phone calls from the nuns at school.

"Emily seems to compulsively repeat everything that's said to her *twice*—once out loud and once under her breath. And she has to tap everything. When the children are supposed to be napping, Emily is up tapping everything in the room."

Same things she was doing at home.

So we took our little space child to be interviewd by three of Boston's finest psychoanalysts to get their expert opinions. In their waiting rooms, Emily wafted about and touched everything twice—doorknobs, magazines, Daddy's shoes, ashtrays, cigarette butts—tap-tap, tap-tap.

"Emotional problems and deep-seated fears" was what two of the three experts came up with. They recommended, of course, that Emily "see somebody."

The third doctor waited a week before getting back to us and when he did, he took our breath away: "It's not autism," he told Sandy on the phone, "but it's in that direction."

Without even discussing it with each other, Sandy and I dismissed this man's diagnosis—because what he'd said was simply *not* acceptable.

To us autism meant hopeless. It meant sitting mute in corners and spinning plates. But Emily talked. And she didn't spin plates.

So instead of focusing on that part of the doctor's sentence that said it's in the *direction* of autism, we focused on the "It's *not* autism..." part.

Therefore, Emily's problem must be something else.
We were right back where we had started.
And that "wind" kept right on blowing.

# – 8 –

# ABBY

*Test pilot radioed back to control tower: "I'm lost, but I'm making record time."*
                                                —*Abraham Maslow*
                          Religions, Values, and Peak Experiences

A little over two years after Emily was born, Abby arrived.

This time there was no haunting, no weird feelings, no chill, no memories, no sense of impending doom.

What happened instead was that I hurt my back.

A week after I got home from the hospital I decided to stain the living room floors a dark Spanish brown. I rented a heavy industrial sander, moved all the furniture aside, stripped down the floor, sanded it, stained it, rented a waxer/polisher and waxed and polished it, then replaced all the furniture. As my last act, I leaned over to lift the couch over the rug—and snap. Into bed I went and finally into traction.

When the "new baby" nurse had to leave for another job, my mother came up from Connecticut to help out. I couldn't move and Mrs. Owens had her hands full with Emily.

"I want to talk to you, Sylvie," my mother said the first time we were alone.

Inside I went "Oh-oh." I knew I wasn't going to come out of this conversation without feeling guilty about something.

"Are you thinking of going back to work after this?" She pointed to the traction equipment. She was leading up to something.

"As soon as I'm better. I can't just stay here."

"Why not? Why can't you be a wife and mother for a while?"

"Because I can't do that," I said impatiently.

"But you just had a baby and now a back injury. Why don't you just take a year or so off? You don't need the money. Why do you *push* yourself so? Why did you have to stain floors right after you'd had a child? What do you need to prove?"

"You don't understand. I have to do things. I go crazy if I don't work. I feel like a nothing if I don't have a title."

"You could do your writing."

"Write about what—motherhood?"

"People do."

"I don't."

"What about your photography?" My mother had been giving all this some thought, that much was clear.

"That's just a hobby."

"But you do such beautiful work."

Now I was angry. "I hate that! I hate it when people tell me that. I don't have to do something just because I'm good at it. I'm good at a lot of things. Sometimes that drives me crazy."

Sandy walked in with a tray. On it was a baby bottle for Abby and a martini for me. His timing was perfect. My stomach was churning. I couldn't wait until that warm ball of golden liquid splashed down over the knot in my insides. I took a huge gulp.

"Don't gulp," my mother said automatically. Ever since I was a little girl, she'd been telling me, "Don't drink so fast, Sylvie. Put your glass down between swallows. You don't have to finish it all at once."

She turned to Sandy.

"Your wife is pushing herself too much. Can't you tell her to slow down?"

My mother would never have taken the conversation this far unless she was feeling helpless to influence me herself.

"She's in some kind of race," Sandy said. (I was surprised he'd given my situation so much thought—even to the point of coming to conclusions.) "She's not going to slow down until she's crossed the finish line—even if she drops dead doing it."

Since the two of them were now having their case conference without me, I proceeded to drink the rest of my martini. When I finished, I held out my glass towards Sandy, indicating that I wanted a refill. Sandy shot me a look; I gave him a "back-off" glare in return. He took the glass and headed for the kitchen.

My mother stood up.

"I'm going to go get Abby. I think she's awake. I'll bring her in. And Sylvia, I think Emily needs a little attention from you, back or no back."

"She crawls up on the bed and it hurts," I said defensively. There it was—the guilt again for being no damn good, for being a doll-murderer.

I reacted by getting even more defensive. "Why don't you go ask *Sandy* to give Emily more attention? Why is it always *me?* Why is it always the mother who's blamed for everything? Is that fair, do you think?"

"I don't know about *fair*. What I do know is what Emily needs." She walked out.

A few minutes later she brought Abby in to me.

Like Emily, Abby was dark-haired, but had large hazel eyes, softer features than Emily's and gave no indication that she'd grow into the doe-eyed beauty she is today. Then she was kind of funny-looking.

I studied her. She had a very wise look. This kid knows something, I said to myself. I think she's on to me!

As I sipped on my second martini (how I hated having to rely on somebody else to bring it to me!) I fed Abby her bottle. We were alone. I began to get sleepy from the drink...

"Hey, wake up, dammit!"

Sandy was yelling at me and when I opened my eyes, he was pulling Abby away from me.

"You might have rolled over on her!" He was angry.

I snapped right back. "Only animals do that!"

"Don't flatter yourself."

Slowly, my back improved. I went from traction to a wheelchair, from a wheelchair to a backbrace *and* a cane to just the backbrace—and that's when I went back to work.

By the time I got home at night I was in a lot of pain which warranted, of course, the best painkiller in the world: gin.

On days I didn't go into the office, I'd write.

And I'd suffer.

Oh, how I'd suffer over writing words down on paper.

For somebody who so far had only been published in high school and college lit magazines, I agonized over writing as if I were actually getting paid for it! I'd pace around and have anxiety attacks and wring my hands like a mourner.

I became a "swamp walker"—one who mucked around in emotional misery.

"If it's that painful, don't write," Sandy would say. It seemed like a reasonable enough suggestion to him.

But it would make me furious. "I can't do that!" I'd shout. "If I don't write, it's worse."

"You're really caught between a rock and a hard place, aren't you?"

Then he'd go to the TV and turn it on.

Then I'd go get a drink—and turn myself *off*.

# – 9 –

# CALIFORNIA DREAMING

*You're not drunk if you can lie on the floor
without holding on.*
— Dean Martin

I thought my destiny as a writer would be to sell sensitive short stories
to *The New Yorker*.

Instead, my first writing sale was an article in *Mademoiselle* called
"How to Stay Sane through *His* Analysis." It was about coping with
your feelings once a husband or boyfriend enters into the mysterious
world of psychotherapy or analysis.

The idea came from the fact that about half the people I knew were
either in therapy themselves or had "significant others" in therapy—or
both—and they had feelings about it.

I interviewed all my psychiatrist and psychologist friends. I interviewed "significant others." I even interviewed Sandy. (What a great
excuse to have an actual conversation with him!) I made an appointment
and went to his office, asked him questions, and wrote down his
answers.

I found out that I liked to interview people.

Back in 1967 an article from the point of view of "significant others"
was unusual. Everything was being written about the patient or "victim." Today, of course, relatives get all kinds of attention. If you're
the second cousin twice removed of a beri-beri victim, there's probably
a support group you can go to and share your feelings.

Being published in a *real* magazine was exciting. It was my initiation
rite.

It made me a *real* writer.

Unfortunately, it didn't do a thing to keep me from continuing on my way towards being a *real* alcoholic.

A few months later I sold another article—this one to *McCall's*. The title makes me wince today but at the time it was an appropriate question: "Should Wives Work?"

Again, I interviewed all my friends and made a good case for a woman's right and need to work. The article struck a nerve and I got hundreds of letters in response to it.

"That makes two article sold," Sandy said at dinner one night (he was doing the eating). "Are you happy?" All he wanted was for me to be happy—just for *once*.

But I couldn't give him that. I couldn't even let myself have that.

I didn't feel comfortable being happy.

I only felt comfortable being a swamp walker.

Sandy's career was moving right along just as mine seemed to be.

More and more he was pulling out in front of the pack and leaving his Freudian-trained colleagues behind. When he saw patients, he often saw them *with* their spouses and family members. He was conducting his practice like a damned social worker!

However, by now his departure from Freud wasn't as distressing because I was starting to go sour on Freud myself. I didn't like Freud's view of women. The women's movement was still underground, but it was in the air. I could feel it and I was primed.

I was a revolutionary just waiting to happen.

Sandy became involved in something called General Systems Theory—another term for what looked to me like social worker stuff (the patient is not isolated but part of a larger system, etc., etc.). He was corresponding with some people in California, which led to his being asked to be a participant on a panel at the upcoming American Psychiatric Association convention in Detroit.

He accepted and I went along.

What Sandy later remembered about Detroit was that it was a career highlight.

What I remember about Detroit was that they didn't serve liquor on Sunday.

After Detroit, Sandy felt he couldn't do business in Boston anymore. "It's a psychoanalytic walled city," he said. "It's getting suffocating."

54

So Sandy flew to Los Angeles, a place we both thought we'd like to live, to see what it was like in terms of work.

"I'll phone you tonight," he said. "I'll call you at eleven o'clock Boston time."

During the evening (Boston time) I drank martinis. I now had a way of preparing them that made it impossible to keep track of how much I was drinking. I'd start out with gin and a dash of vermouth on the rocks. Then I'd add another ice cube, next a little gin, another ice cube, a sprinkle of vermouth—a dash more gin.

It was hard to tell where one drink left off and the next began. It was all one long drink—like the knife story: If you have a knife and the handle breaks and you get a new handle, and then later on if the blade breaks and you get a new blade, is it the same knife? or a different knife?

That was my martini.

At about nine o'clock that night, the girls safely in bed, I remember walking into the bathroom, looking down at the white fuzzy rug and thinking how nice it would be to lie down on it just for a little while. So I did.

When I woke up, I was still there.

My first thought was, "Sandy's phone call."

I ran into the bedroom to look at the clock—two o'clock in the morning! I'd missed his call!

I went into a tailspin. How was I going to get out of this one?

I decided to tell Sandy a lie—a bigger lie than the one about eating lunch late.

"The phone was out of order," I told him when he called the next day, even before he'd had a chance to ask me why I hadn't answered it.

There was silence on the other end. Then he said: "What are you talking about, out of order? The phone wasn't out of order. You answered and we had a whole conversation."

I went clammy inside: caught!

Nanci Dean, the patient at Boston State, flashed through my mind: Is this what she meant by Swiss cheese nights?

That scared me.

I didn't touch gin for the rest of the two weeks that Sandy was in L.A.

And I didn't sleep much either. I was jumpy and nervous. I didn't know I was experiencing withdrawal. Again I chalked it up to being so sensitive and deep. I stayed up, cleaned out closets and files, and went through old magazines before throwing them out. In one of them I ran across an article called "Are You An Alcoholic?" I flipped the page quickly. That's got nothing to do with *me*, I said to myself.

During staff meetings at work I had the same strange reaction to the word "alcoholic"—avoidance. I tuned out saying, "That's got nothing to do with me."

Why was I so uncomfortable?

When Sandy got back from Los Angeles, I was beginning to sleep better (the worst of the withdrawal being over) and I was feeling surprisingly good.

Maybe I just needed a break from marriage I concluded. It didn't dawn on me that feeling good was related to *not* drinking gin.

Neither of us mentioned the phone call incident. And of course, since I'd been off drinking, I'd been conscious for all Sandy's other calls—which helped make up for it.

I felt virtuous for going two weeks without drinking (somebody who could do that obviously didn't have a "problem"). I decided to celebrate by having a drink with Sandy at the airport while he told me about his adventures in the land of the sun. I sipped at it daintily; I didn't get snarly at all.

I handled it so well, in fact, that I had no qualms about fixing a martini the following evening. That was Monday.

By Wednesday I had another Swiss cheese night.

"I didn't like what you said to me at dinner," Sandy told me at breakfast.

Oh, God, I thought. Did we have a fight? I scurried around my brain like a rat looking for a way out.

Then I had it!

"What *part* of what I said last night didn't you like?" I said—cleverly, I thought.

"The part about psychiatry being a Mickey-Mouse profession." Sandy fell right into my trap and provided me with the information I needed. "You generalize too much."

I gave him what I hoped was a properly chagrined look, "Sorry."

"Okay," he said.

Sandy passed his California medical boards to get his California medical license and landed a job as an administrator of a community mental health clinic just south of Los Angeles. He was still nervous about working with patients directly, still not willing to get back on the horse. So, our move to California was on. That was good.

I was counting on California. Now everything that had gone wrong would be better.

I threw myself into the preparations for the move.

Sandy came home one day to find me painting the baseboards in the living room.

"They were all chipped," I said. "I don't want anybody to think we were slobs."

My mother was upset. She didn't want us to go away. She didn't want to be so far away from her grandchildren. But she, as ever, remained stoic. On one of our last visits to Connecticut, I caught tears in her blue-blue eyes as she held on to Emily and rocked her. I think she was worried about what would become of this strange child under my ambivalent mothering in California.

I remember feeling nothing—nothing about seeing my mother's tears, nothing about leaving my friends, nothing about leaving everything I'd known. I just turned my back on it all and left and didn't even miss anybody. I thought this was a tribute to my progress, my maturity.

I didn't know until years later when I began to feel again that what *that* was all about wasn't maturity, it was gin.

Gin had made my feelings for people go dead.

Sandy, the kids, Mrs. Owens the nurse (she'd decided to move along with us) and the two cats went by plane.

All our furniture went by moving van.

And I went by train.

My plane phobia had returned.

"You used to fly when we were dating," Sandy said, puzzled.

"I can only fly when I'm in love," I shot back.

Sandy was silent for a moment. "Thanks a lot," he said.

On the train to Los Angeles, I felt peace. I felt safe. Nobody could reach me here. It was like those times in my life when I'd "disappeared"—under the surface of the lake as a kid; up on the hill in Connecticut before my marriage to Lucas; into myself sitting on the edge of the bathtub before my marriage to Sandy. And now on the train to Los Angeles—four whole days of being *gone*.

After the stop-over in Chicago, I sat in the bar car with a book and a martini. When it got crowded, I was joined by a woman who was to become my friend and drinking companion, Veda.

Veda was Hungarian, glamorous and funny. She was returning to Los Angeles from a "tryst" in Washington, D.C., with a married congressman.

She liked to drink.

After our third or fourth drink, she began to ask me questions. "Darling"—she actually said Darling to people—"tell me all about your husband."

"He thinks I drink too much." I told her that without meaning to. It just fell out.

"Ridiculous!" Veda protested. "You don't drink any more than I do."

That made me feel better.

Just then the train lurched and I spilled some of my martini on my hand. Automatically I licked it off instead of wiping it off with a napkin.

Veda caught that and winked at me. We both laughed.

It was the first time I didn't feel uncomfortable about my drinking. After all, who was she to judge?

I liked being with someone who had no right to judge.

"Now, what's this woman's thing you were telling me about?" Veda asked. "It sounds fascinating."

"Women's rights."

"Oh? I thought we already had our rights."

"I can see I'm going to have to educate you."

"Okay, darling. Shoot."

I told her all about the article I'd just read in the *New York Times Magazine* that made the women's liberation movement a reality for me. Women, I told Veda, are still being badly discriminated against.

"Not me!" Veda said. "A *man* is paying for this trip. You're going to tell me that hurts me?"

"But you're paying a price for that, Veda!"

"Such as?"

"Maybe you can *sleep* with a congressman—but just try to *be* one!"

"No thank you, darling!" She laughed her full, rich laugh. She was enjoying this little debate. "I absolutely couldn't imagine anything worse! Let him have the ulcer and let me have the trip!"

She ordered us both another drink.

I'd never had anybody order a drink for me without my having to ask for it or offer a reason why I needed it. It was a relief!

When the drinks came, she gulped at hers and gazed out at the summer evening landscape as we sped across America.

"Sweetheart!" she said. "I have a wonderful idea. You must come to my little house in Cheviot Hills. My husband left it to me when he died. You'll simply love it. And I'll make you my Hungarian goulash and we will talk about all these rights you want for women. Okay?"

I nodded—but thought I should warn her.

"I'd love to come but I'm afraid I almost never eat dinner. I wouldn't want you to go to all that trouble for nothing."

"My darling, I *never* eat dinner but I *always* cook my goulash anyway because it smells so divine!"

Veda took another gulp of her Scotch and I could tell just by watching her that she had a really *serious* drinking problem—just like Faye—and that was the main difference between us.

I felt badly that Veda, like Faye, had been hit with one of Aristotle's arrows.

If I ever drink like that, I said to myself, then I'll begin to worry.

# – 10 –

# PANDORA'S BOX

*No wind favors a ship without a destination.*
*—Seneca, first century A.D.*

Sandy picked me up at Union Station and drove me back to our new home, a lovely two-story Spanish sublet in Westwood near UCLA. The girls and Mrs. Owens had their own wing.

The master bedroom was large, so large I turned half of it into an office. I planned to write full-time and leave psychology behind—my protest against its anti-female stance.

Coming from cities (Boston and New York) I had all the typical reactions to Los Angeles—like where the hell *is* it? Where's the hub, the center, the place where the action is?

I never could figure out when people worked. In Boston the week divided up neatly into workdays, 9-5, and weekends. L.A. was all one twenty-four-hour happening. And in spite of morning and evening traffic jams on the freeways, there seemed to be as many people left behind as going.

I felt like Alice in Wonderland after the shrinking medicine—everything seemed big. Freeway on-ramps were big. The fruits and vegetables from the truck that came around twice a week were big. The snails in the garden were big.

We settled in.

Sandy commuted to his new job and I got down to work on a third article assignment—again, for *McCall's*.

Mrs. Owens, always in a starched, white uniform, created a tiny, structured universe for the girls, who had just turned two and four. Get up. Get dressed. Breakfast. Watch *Sesame Street*. Play in the new sandbox. Wash up. Lunch. Nap. Take a nice walk. Bath. Supper. Story. Kiss Mommy and Daddy goodnight. Bed.

I had very little to do with any of it, except on weekends when Mrs. Owens would retire to her rooms and write her letters home to Boston.

On weekends I was nervous. I knew I was supposed to love being with my children, watching them grow, but I didn't. Reading stories and playing blocks was torture for me; it wasn't "accomplishing" anything. I was only comfortable when I was working.

As Abby and Emily got older, the difference between them became more apparent. Abby was definitely of this world, definitely "with it"; her lovely hazel eyes were sharp and aware. Intelligence seemed to exude out of them. Emily on the other hand was in some other world, her eyes dreamy and distant, her speech sometimes strange but her perceptions eerily intuitive: "Lori says she's my friend but her face doesn't look like a friend and my stomach doesn't feel friendly."

Walking into a room, Emily had trouble getting the big picture of what was going on, couldn't connect the parts to the whole. Her world seemed a jumble of overstimulating, disconnected fragments that made no sense and sometimes she appeared overwhelmed, frightened and had to tune things out to protect herself, including me: "When you make a loud voice I can't hear you."

We took Emily to "see somebody," just as the Boston shrinks had suggested. We got a referral from one of them to a Freudian-trained (what else?) woman (at least *that*) psychiatrist whose operating principle was that Emily was merely "disturbed" and play therapy would fix it.

I paid lip service to the idea but I didn't really buy it.

I'd lost the faith.

I, too, no longer believed in psychiatrists—which for me was like a Catholic losing faith in God.

It made me feel very, very much alone.

I resented having to take Emily to useless appointments in the middle of a week day when I had work to do. I resented it even more after Dr. Yonan began asking me questions like "did I drink" which I denied, denied, denied. Finally, on some pretext, I got Mrs. Owens to go with Emily instead of me.

Sandy and I fought over everything. I rarely stopped to wonder how we got to this awful place from where we'd started. I certainly never connected it to chemicals—the pills or the drinking.

I'd practically stopped eating. Breakfast consisted of coffee, cigarettes (I'd now reached two packs a day) and a Dexedrine to help me write. More coffee and cigarettes while I worked—and maybe another half a Dexedrine. Then a yogurt or cookie for lunch. Gin and cigarettes for dinner. And a Valium or Nembutal—or both—at night to help me sleep.

I got thinner and thinner.

"You look like something out of Dachau," my sister Justine had said to me when she came out for a visit.

Occasionally Sandy and I would attempt a restaurant dinner. My intentions to behave and eat were always good. I'd get all dressed up (carrying my "get-dressed" martini around with me) and off we'd go.

At the restaurant Sandy would ask me (as if he didn't know) if I'd like a cocktail. I'd say, "A martini, please." Then Sandy would repeat what I'd just said to the waiter: "The lady will have a martini."

"He *heard* me!" I'd say under my breath, gritting my teeth.

"What was *that* all about?" Sandy would say as soon as the waiter left.

"Why do waiters only talk to *men*? Don't women exist?"

"It's just tradition that the man orders."

"It's like being at the United Nations—I say something and you have to translate for the damned waiter."

"Don't take it so personally," Sandy would say.

"It bothers me."

"*Everything* bothers you."

Then I'd pout (with or without tears sliding down my face) and the rest of the meal would be ruined. I'd sit there and use "being upset" as my excuse to keep on drinking and not eat the expensive meal as Sandy munched away. Nothing ever kept Sandy from eating.

"I want another martini."

"That's your third."

"You're counting," I'd say, meaning "lay off."

Mrs. Owens should probably have structured my little universe, as well as the girls', because once I'd finished the *McCall's* article assignment, I ran dry. I didn't know what else to write about.

My ideas had been coming from being *out there* and now that I was stuck in this big house in this big state of California with a two-year-old, a Martian, a nursemaid, a depressed psychiatrist and gin, I had nothing to say.

I got into procrastinations (shades of my stepfather) and even into a form of "estate-walking" (I'd lie in the sun in different places in the backyard), all the while getting a bigger and bigger knot in my stomach so I couldn't wait until five o'clock—or four o'clock—or three-thirty.

I was at loose ends.

At such a time another woman might have taken on a lover.

Not I.

What I did was take on a revolution.

After reading the *New York Times* article about the new feminist wave, I'd written a letter to the National Organization for Women (NOW) requesting information. It was the first I'd heard of NOW.

When the NOW material arrived, I took it out in the backyard with me to read while I sat in the sun.

What I read excited me.

I devoured every word. I read and re-read NOW's statement of goals and purposes, the history, the statistics ("By God, I *am* being discriminated against! I *knew* it!"), the committees one could join. My heart was pounding. I felt insatiable. It was like a drug I couldn't get enough of. I wanted more to read—so I read the names of the board members, information about where the material was printed and even the postmark!

All I could think was "I'm home."

I read that NOW's second annual convention was coming up soon in Atlanta, Georgia. Betty Friedan, NOW's founding mother and author of *The Feminine Mystique*, would be there.

I knew somebody else who would be there.

*Me*.

"You're *flying* to Atlanta? I thought you could only fly when you're in love." Sandy was finding it increasingly difficult to figure me out.

I didn't understand it, either. All I knew was that my flying phobia had once again disappeared, chased away by a cause, by an overwhelming idea larger than myself that seemed to be pulling me forward, an idea so strong that it could keep airplanes up in the air.

It was *like* being in love.

# – 11 –

# WHAT DID YOU DO
# IN THE WAR, MOMMY?

*There is no safety in numbers or anything else.*
*—James Thurber*

*Atlanta, Georgia:* Barely one hundred people squeezed into the tiny hotel conference room for the September, 1968, annual convention of the National Organization for Women—fifteen of the one hundred were press.

Women's liberation was hardly a household word—yet.

I recognized Betty Friedan with Coretta Scott King at her side. They were just finishing a press conference.

It was heady stuff.

I eavesdropped on an intense, animated dialogue between Betty Friedan and two other women—should this NOW convention tackle the sticky question of women and the draft?

I was filled with anticipation. It was a good feeling to discover that all those secret "crazy" thoughts I'd been having about the plight of women weren't so crazy after all. They were valid. I remembered all those times my psychiatrist in Boston had pointed out to me that my "problem" was my neurotic inability to accept my role—he actually said that! And yet standing there that day it was clear to me this was no mental health issue we were dealing with—this was a *social* issue, a political issue.

It was okay to take it seriously.

That was my first lesson.

My second lesson was that the worst male chauvinists are women. The word comes from the legendary French soldier in Napoleon's army, Nicholas Chauvin, who went so overboard in his worship of Napoleon that he was considered a fool.

I discovered this during the first two minutes of the keynote address when a woman approached the podium and I assumed she was there to introduce the *male* speaker who would enlighten us about our oppression! As it began to dawn on me that she was *it*—the speaker—my first reaction was disappointment; I didn't even want to listen.

That's when I caught myself: *I'm* the one with the prejudice! I almost blushed out loud.

Lesson number three was discovering what my own personal mission in this movement would be: help awaken women to the existence of the male chauvinist within.

For so many of us, especially the brand new ones like me, this NOW convention was a catharsis. We dumped years of pent-up feelings. We talked and talked—and then talked some more. It was a gushing forth—we were geysers. There seemed to be no end to all we had to say.

I began to understand something about causes: You don't choose a cause—it chooses you. For years I'd felt guilty for not picketing for or against something the way friends of mine had. And then women's lib fell into my lap and it was *my* cause, *my* battle, not somebody else's, not a second-hand cause, but *mine*.

If my life up to now had been a movie—and if, in the story, beginning success as a writer hadn't "cured" my drinking and pilling, then surely finding a cause would!

But no such luck.

Addiction doesn't work like that.

Addiction has a life of its own and skips along oblivious to what its "host" is doing. Addiction doesn't pay attention to what your goals in life are and whether or not you've fulfilled them. Addiction doesn't care if you're happy or down-and-out. Addiction wants only that which it is addicted to—or it'll break your leg!

So towards the end of that first exciting day in Atlanta, as the clock crept towards five o'clock, the little addict inside of me wanted satisfaction. I grudgingly went out to a coffee shop with two other women who were from Los Angeles—I didn't eat much—and I toughed it out until I could get to my room, pull the bottle of gin out of my suitcase, and do what I had to do.

The next morning I was hung over, but I was used to that and medicated myself with a Valium for the shakiness (I still figured this was "nerves") and later in the morning, half a Dexedrine to stay awake because the Valium made me sleepy.

Lots of coffee during the day and another half a Dexedrine in the p.m.

The second day was even more exciting as I began to feel more and more a part of this thing. I'd discovered there was a monthly NOW meeting in Los Angeles and I knew I'd be a regular.

At the end of the day, Sunday, Betty Friedan announced an open house cocktail party in her suite upstairs to say goodbye.

Of course I went.

And of course I drank. Fast. Gulping.

We crowded into Betty's suite and spilled out into the hallway. I sat on the edge of one of the beds and shared more sexist "war stories." I was having a splendid time—and every once in a while I'd get up and get another drink.

We made plans to have a perfect world.

Meanwhile, my speech was becoming less perfect. I began to slur my words and stumble over my "s's", so I had to think of replacement words for the "s" sound. I started to slur the word "sexist" and changed it to "male chauvinist," which was a bit easier. It was frustrating because I *wanted* to stay there and talk. I *needed* to talk. But my inner addict had other plans.

I knew I was drunk. But did *they* know I was drunk? Did Betty Friedan know I was drunk? That's what bothered me the most—if she could see it. I wanted her approval. I wanted to be a part of this thing. I didn't want to humiliate myself but I was setting about to do just that.

Fortunately, I had a case of "Faye's rays" and something inside of me stood me up and walked me out of the room, down the hall and down two flights of stairs and into my own room where I closed the door, lunged into the bathroom, lifted up the toilet seat, bent down before it on my knees on the cold tile floor, and threw up.

Then I got up, walked over to the bed, lay down on it fully dressed, shoes and all, and passed out.

Whatever the other ninety-nine people from the convention did that night, I wasn't a part of it. I wanted to be a part of it—but because I had to answer to a higher authority, I wasn't able to be.

On the flight back to L.A. the next day I made several round trips to the ladies' room so I could drain the little bottled martinis I'd bought at the airport. This, in addition to the two drinks I ordered from my seat. I was convinced the plane was falling down so the drinks proved my theory: Gin keeps airplanes up in the air.

Sandy picked me up from the airport, expecting a wife.
What he got was a tipsy revolutionary.

# – 12 –

# FRONT LINES

*Everybody thinks of changing humanity and nobody thinks of changing himself.*

—*Leo Tolstoy*

I jumped right into the revolution.

In those early days of NOW, we were so small in number that anybody who was a squeaky wheel was oiled and put to work.

I became a very squeaky wheel.

When I found out that there had been a monthly NOW meeting in Los Angeles only a few miles from my house and I hadn't even heard about it, I made a fuss:

"How do you expect people to join the revolution if they can't *find* it?" I said in a phone call to a woman named Toni who was then president of the Southern California NOW chapter. "Are we a secret?"

"What do you suggest?" she said.

"We need to be listed with Information. We need to be in the phone book. We need an answering service. We need a mailing address. We need brochures. We need stationery."

I discovered that fledgling movements have very little red tape.

"Fine," she said. "Go right ahead."

So the Southern California chapter of NOW got a phone number (my house) and an answering service with mailing address. I pasted up some stationery and had it run off at a local printer. Then I sat down at my kitchen table with another NOW member and we wrote up a statistics sheet about the status of women called "Vive la Difference?" We used press-on letters for the title, put our new address and phone number at the bottom, had a few hundred run off, and we were in business.

"We need a newsletter," I said, "so we can communicate with each other locally and with other chapters nationally and even with other liberation groups."

"Fine," Toni said. "Go right ahead."

So I started a newsletter for the Southern California chapter. In the beginning, I got to write it, edit it, type it, paste it up, take the photos for it, take it to the printer, collate it, staple it, type out the labels for it, stamp it, fold it and mail it out.

I was spending everything I got from Sandy and what little I got from my writing on the movement.

"We need publicity," was my next bright idea. "We need newspaper and magazine interviews. We need to go on the radio, on TV talk shows, spread the word."

"Fine," Toni said. "I appoint you an official spokeswoman for NOW. You can start handling the media whenever you wish."

In 1968, the idea of "handling the media" was funny. *What* media? Most of the media hadn't heard of us and when I phoned up to tell them all about it, they said "So what?" There were too many other things, important things, to cover like the black movement and Vietnam. We were still "women's pages" stuff.

Two years later, of course, when "Women's Lib" hit the cover of *Time* magazine, it would be a whole different story. But in the meantime, our coverage came in dribs and drabs. It was clear that we were going to have to come up with something a bit dramatic if we wanted to attract the press.

The issue chosen was this: across the nation NOW chapters would picket any major newspapers that still divided their want-ads into Help Wanted: Male and Help Wanted: Female.

I'd become such a squeaky wheel in Los Angeles that Betty Friedan heard me herself three thousand miles away in New York.

One morning I got a long-distance phone call from Betty's office: "Betty wants you to write the press releases for the *Los Angeles Times* want-ads demonstration," her assistant Dolores Alexander said.

"Dolores, I don't know *how* to write a press release! I've never written a press release in my life. I don't even know what one *looks* like."

I expected to be let off the hook immediately.

But that's not what happened. "Betty says you'll learn," Dolores said.

That was Betty Friedan's credo—Learn by doing.

She wanted us to stop bitching about how this sexist culture had never taught us women any skills and start learning these skills by grabbing opportunities like this when they were offered. "Jump in and learn," she said, "or shut up!"

So I learned.

I went to the library and checked out books on journalism and read up on how to write a press release. I called up a couple of journalists I knew and had them scrounge around for sample press releases so I could copy from them. I boned up on all the facts and stats related to the planned demonstration and then three of us from NOW met with *Los Angeles Times* officials face to face (including their lawyer) to let them know what we were up to—and, of course, give them a chance to "desegregate" their want-ads before we picketed (which they didn't do).

From all this, I finally managed to create a two-page press release. Those five hundred words or less had taken me two weeks!

I sent copies to Betty Friedan and Dolores Alexander.

"That's fine," was all Dolores said. But it was enough. It meant I had learned a new skill!

Betty Friedan seemed tireless, unrelenting. And since there were still so few of us worker-bees in NOW, she was forced to put us all to overwork. It didn't matter how many other tasks we were already performing, Betty had more for us to do.

I was appointed to the national board of NOW and began flying to meetings in different cities—New York, San Francisco, New Orleans, San Diego—in planes kept airborne by gin. Betty Friedan was always there with assignments. Already into overload, I took to hiding behind hotel lobby pillars or camouflaging myself in crowds so she wouldn't notice me and nail me with another job. I don't think it was personal with her. I doubt she even remembered my name from meeting to meeting. It's just that anyone she caught moving, she'd nab. So the best escape was freeze. Avoid eye contact. Play dead.

Once in the lobby of a San Francisco hotel I wasn't quick enough and Betty got me.

"Come out here," she said, waving me to follow her as she sailed through the revolving door and out onto the street and into a taxi that was waiting at the curb. Inside the taxi was another NOW member who'd been similarly kidnapped.

I climbed in, the door was slammed shut and we sped off to a destination unknown.

We ended up at a radio station where Betty was interviewed. All she'd wanted was company on the way and a little moral support while she was on the air. But she was usually too focused on her task to take time out to explain these things to you. After the interview we got another cab back to the hotel—and then Betty let us go.

The more I learned about the role of women in our culture, the more I was convinced that *that* was why I wasn't happy. Only when women have their rights, I decided, will I be okay. If the world isn't okay, how can *I* be okay?

It made perfect sense to me.

So seven days a week I labored to make the world a fit place for me to live in.

And seven nights a week I got drunk.

Meanwhile Emily the Martian had taken to wafting around the big house and sliding material things out of open windows: clothes, silverware, jewelry, toys, magazines, can openers, food—*out* the window. If something was missing, it could usually be found in the bushes around the house.

Once I found Emily standing at the bathroom sink in the dark with the faucet running full blast. "I can't see this water in here," she explained. "I think it's a ghost."

She had her whimsical moments.

Sandy did everything he knew how to do to make me happy. He even joined NOW (we had male members).

He believed in the women's movement. He had a strong inner sense of justice, of what's fair. And women's liberation was fair.

But there were limitations to his enthusiasm for revolution as a steady diet.

One early evening when it was still warm and light, I was out on the lawn (martini close by) making picket signs for the upcoming *Times* demonstration. Emily and Abby were bopping around the lawn with Mrs. Owens. Sandy was stretched out on a deck chair by the pool, reading his "sexist establishment psychiatric propaganda" as I called it.

"Which sign do I have to carry?" Sandy asked.

"The one that says 'Friend of Women.'"

"I'm going to feel like an ass."

"Sandy, you promised!"

"I did. But this isn't my thing. This is *your* thing."

"Discrimination against women hurts you, too," I said.

"Not that I've noticed so far."

"That was a male chauvinist pig kind of crack."

"I *am* a male chauvinist pig."

"Why do men always think it's cute to say that? You wouldn't think saying you were a racist was cute."

"I kind of like things the way they are." He was toying with me now.

"It's not fair the way they are."

"If they get fair," Sandy said, "I lose."

"Will you shut up!" I had no humor anymore. It was down at the bottom of a bottle somewhere. I had a short fuse.

I walked over to the very edge of the pool.

"What are you doing?" Sandy sensed that I was up to something.

"I'm going down to the bottom where it's quiet and stay there," I said.

Then I jumped into the pool with my clothes on. I swam down to the bottom and began to scream and as I did so huge bubbles swept past my face and rose to the top. I swam around underwater until my lungs felt about to burst and then I surfaced.

Sandy was gone.

Mrs. Owens and the girls were way down at the other end of the lawn, picking flowers.

My little drama had had no audience.

I got out of the pool and walked into the kitchen dripping wet. Sandy was at the kitchen table.

"You promised me you'd stay down there," he said.

I didn't answer.

I deliberately poured myself a big drink right in front of his face. I felt like it was a weapon.

"What do you need that stuff for?"

I didn't like that word, need. "I don't *need* it. I *want* it."

Somehow that seemed to make a difference.

I took the drink into the living room and lay down on the couch in my wet clothes—and passed out.

My tolerance was decreasing, so it was taking less and less gin to do more and more damage.

I woke up at midnight. I was still on the couch in cold, damp clothes. I crept upstairs, got undressed and into bed.

Sandy was asleep.

"You fell asleep on the couch with your cigarette burning last night," Sandy said the next morning. "You could have burned the house down."

I was quiet a moment. "I've been thinking of quitting," I said.

"Drinking?"

"No, smoking."

The *Los Angeles Times* want-ad demonstration went well. We got the news coverage we so badly needed.

Sandy and I were invited to be interviewed the following day on a local noon news show. Sandy even took the afternoon off from work.

He did beautifully. He was billed as a "pro-feminist psychiatrist married to an active feminist."

I was hungover and shaky.

After showing a film clip of Sandy picketing with his "Friend of Women" sign in the demonstration, the interviewer asked him questions.

"As a psychiatrist, what do you think of the women's liberation movement, doctor?"

"My being a psychiatrist is irrelevant," Sandy said. "The women's movement is a social issue, not a mental health issue. Women really *are* discriminated against. That's fact. So you can't say that any woman who feels discriminated against is exhibiting pathology. She's not sick."

"So you yourself don't feel threatened by women's lib, doctor?"

"Not at all. It's potentially the best thing that ever happened to men. After all, we're put into niches and forced to play roles, too. The pressures on men to perform, make money, and be strong are fierce. I see the casualties in my private practice all the time—stress, ulcers, depression, sleeplessness, divorce."

The interviewer asked me a few questions, but Sandy was definitely the star of this show. The segment ended when the interviewer said to me, "Sounds like you two have a pretty good thing going." Then he said right into the camera: "Now maybe some of you women out there—and men, too—can ask yourself this question: 'How equal is *your* marriage?'"

"You did great!" I bubbled to Sandy on the way home. "I was so impressed! I didn't know you'd learned all that."

"That was my last performance," he said. "I'm bowing out. I've got better things to do. From now on you fight your own battles."

"What do you mean, 'better' things to do?"

"I've got my *work* to do, for one thing."

"Psychiatry? Psychiatry that puts down women and calls it mental health? That's 'better'?"

"Some people have problems other than not getting equal pay for equal work, you know," Sandy said. He was not in a good mood.

"Psychiatry," I said, aiming for the jugular, "is shit!"

Sandy didn't answer right away. The expression on his face was strained. When he spoke it was very soft, very controlled: "If you don't shut up," he said, "I'm going to stop this car and slug you."

I said no more all the way home. I actually did feel badly for my remark about psychiatry, but since I couldn't handle being wrong about anything I couldn't apologize, so I let it go.

When we got back to the house, the girls were still napping and Mrs. Owens was in her room.

Sandy went for the icebox and got out some celery which he neatly cut up and put on a paper plate.

I looked at the clock. Only 2:30. Damn! Too early to make a drink.

"I'm going upstairs," Sandy said as he grabbed the salt shaker.

"Good. And you can take your damn celery with you!"

I went into the living room and put some records on the stereo. The first one that dropped was "Judy Blue Eyes" by Crosby, Stills, and Nash: "—I am me, you are you, you are what you are—but you make it so hard-ar-ar-ar-ard. But you make it so hard-ar-ar-ar-ard—"

I sat on the couch and began to cry. I felt isolated, desolate, abandoned, suicidal.

What is happening to me? I thought. Why does everything hurt so much?

They were questions I couldn't answer.

So I just sat there very still and waited for five o'clock.

# – 13 –

## MEN DON'T CRY

*Those who have given themselves the most concern about the happiness of peoples have made their neighbors very miserable.*

—Anatole France
The Crime of Sylvestre Bonnard

When our lease was up on the Westwood sublet, we bought a house in Brentwood north of Sunset. Sandy's parents kicked in the $80,000 down payment as a gift—which I hardly even bothered to appreciate. When it came to things financial, I was oblivious. Any time Sandy tried to explain something practical to me, I got sleepy.

It was another two-story Spanish house with balconies and bougainvillea, a long gravel driveway that circled a huge fountain surrounded by birds of paradise (my least favorite flower). There was a romantic, grotto-like pool in the midst of well-tended tropical plants.

It made an impressive setting for the press reception that the Southern California chapter of NOW had for Betty Friedan when she was in Los Angeles on a public relations visit.

It also made a peaceful backdrop for my increasingly chaotic life.

There were so many people around, but I had no friends, no one I talked to about anything personal. In NOW, we only talked revolution. And at home, there was Mrs. Owens, the gardener (three times a week), the pool man (twice a week), the maid (once a week) and delivery people up the kazoo. It was like a hotel. I hid in my little office at the foot of the circular stairway and wouldn't come out until everybody had gone away.

One evening, a week after we moved in, Sandy and I went out to sit by the pool. Again, Sandy was reading his shrink journals.

77

"It says here that the American Psychiatric Association has officially labeled alcoholism a *disease*," he suddenly said.

"Oh?" Now why was he telling me this? He didn't tell me the latest scoop on manic-depressive psychosis, so why this?

"That's stupid," Sandy went on. "Alcoholism is just a *habit*."

"Oh."

I felt strangely relieved. I remember thinking, oh, is that all it is? That's not so terrible. And he must know—he's a shrink.

I went back to my reading.

"It also says—" Sandy wasn't about to let this go, "it also says that women are more susceptible to cirrhosis of the liver than men are, especially if they don't eat properly." He looked up at me. "You should make sure you eat properly."

I had an immediate comeback:

"I bet that article was written by a *male* doctor!"

When Sandy's nose was back in his journal, I got up and moved my act inside. I made another drink and went upstairs to the bedroom.

Sandy was unusually quiet the next morning and I was unusually irritable. I ended up throwing my hairbrush across the room after it got tangled in my long hair.

I could hear Abby fussing in her room across the hall.

"Where *is* Mrs. Owens?!" I said angrily.

Sandy said nothing.

"Why are *you* so quiet this morning?" I said.

"What do you want me to say?"

"I don't know! I feel ugly. Tell me I look nice."

"You look nice," Sandy said mechanically.

"You don't mean that. You never just spontaneously say anything nice to me anymore. You never even make love to me anymore." Then I added, challengingly, "How come you stopped making love to me?"

Sandy looked taken aback.

"What about last night?" he said.

I was still up on my high horse: "What are you talking about, last night?"

"You fell asleep on me when I was in the middle of making love to you, don't you remember?"

Caught again! I didn't remember a thing.

"Of course I do, it's just that that doesn't count because I was too tired."

Lies. Lies.

"It didn't do much for my ego. You made me feel like a pretty lousy lover. I've never put anybody to sleep before. I had dreams of being a wet noodle all night, and I don't think a psychiatrist would have too much trouble interpreting that one."

How was I going to get out of this?

Sandy was sitting on the edge of the bed and I walked over to him. I put my hands on his shoulders and looked into his eyes and said: "I'm sorry."

Relief flooded across his face. He *wanted* to make up. He didn't want to fight.

I reached down and touched his fly and he immediately got aroused. Seconds later he'd closed and locked the bedroom door and we were in bed.

NOW's next attention-getting demonstration was, of all things, a bar sit-in at the fancy Polo Lounge of the Beverly Hills Hotel protesting their rule that unescorted women couldn't be served at the bar—the assumption being, of course, that an unescorted woman at a bar is up to no good.

Discrimination! we cried. Unescorted *men* were served, so unescorted women should be served, too. Fair's fair.

I was one of the official spokeswomen for the event. I'd written press releases (by now I was an old hand at it) and they'd worked.

We got coverage.

Two of us were interviewed on an afternoon TV talk show just before the sit-in—and there were cameras as we sidled up to the bar.

When the cameras left and the sit-in was over, I was still sitting on my bar stool. A man appeared on the seat next to me and offered to buy me a drink. He asked me questions about the demonstrations. Then he bought me another drink and asked me more questions.

Suddenly I got hit with "Faye's rays"—those inner warning signals. I knew I had to get out of there. These days two drinks could knock me flat and the thought that here I was, representing NOW, and in the process of getting drunk and being picked up by a man at the bar, just might not look too good considering the thrust of this particular demonstration!

I excused myself and left.

Fortunately, like Cinderella, I didn't turn into a pumpkin until I was on my way home in the car. Then drunkenness hit me.

I weaved along Sunset Boulevard, scared I'd be arrested for drunk driving—which wouldn't look good either.

I was so relieved to make it home without incident that I rushed right into the kitchen and made a drink.

The following week everything I'd told that man at the bar was written up in a negative article about the demonstration in a local underground newspaper.

He'd been a reporter.


Sandy's parents flew out from New York, eager to see the new house and their granddaughters and enjoy a week-long holiday in the California sun.

On their first night in Los Angeles they took us to, of all places, the Beverly Hills Hotel for dinner.

I wondered if I'd be recognized as that troublemaker from NOW, but I wasn't. Yesterday's news is yesterday's news.

After two martinis I was well on my way.

I began to get scrappy with Sandy's father—the same man who had just given us $80,000, no strings attached.

"Arnold," I said. "You and Hedy always ask Sandy about *his* work, but you never ask me about mine. Don't you think I *do* anything?"

And it went downhill from there.

At first Sandy's mother tried to humor me. After a while she'd had enough.

"Arnold, I want to leave!"

Hedy gathered up her things and pushed back her chair.

"Now you've done it!" Sandy said to me. He'd never looked so angry.

I got scared right away.

But there was no stopping his parents. Arnold rose, said goodnight to Sandy and they left.

Immediately I began to defend myself.

"I'm tired of always having to play the good-wife, good-mother role in front of them!" I said, desperate to find some sort of explanation for what I'd just done. "That's all they ever want to hear. They don't even *know* me. I'm a person too!"

"I think they may have gotten to know you too well." With that, Sandy stood up to leave.

"Where are you going!"

"Home."

"Sandy! Don't leave me here!"

"Give me a reason not to."

I was whipped. I couldn't pretend anymore tonight. "Because I'm drunk. I'm too drunk to get up and walk out of here with you. So please don't leave."

"You did this to yourself."

And he walked away.

"Please!"

It did no good.

I couldn't believe he'd done that—just walked out and left me. I didn't even have any money.

I sat there hanging onto the edge of the table as the dining room and I spun through space. I didn't know what to do when a waiter headed my way, so I buried my head in my arms like an ostrich. Maybe if I couldn't see him he couldn't see me.

That's when Sandy came back and rescued me.

Later he told me he'd never really left. He'd stood at the door and watched me suffer for a while. Only when he thought I'd had enough did he return.

"How did you get me out of there?" I asked him the next morning.

"Carried you."

"Did people see?"

"They did."

I cringed inside.

"What about your parents?"

"They flew back to New York this morning."

"They left?"

Sandy nodded. "I think you owe them an apology."

For once I wasn't on the defensive. There was no way I could defend what I'd done, so I stopped trying—and actually, it was kind of a relief.

"I'll write them a letter today," I said simply.

And then I began to weep. The tears just began to flow out of me as though a tap had been gently turned on. I didn't require any comforting—the tears were comfort enough. And Sandy sensed this. I wept and wept and Sandy just sat patiently and watched me.

I was experiencing, I realize now, a moment of "reachability." Maybe, had just the "right" words (whatever they were) been said to me, it might have been a turning point.

"Sandy, what's wrong with me?" I asked. I really did want to know. "I didn't used to be like this. What happened?"

But Sandy had no words, no answers. He, for whatever reasons, wasn't ready to play his part. Instead, an annoyed look crossed his face. I got hurt immediately and my wall came clanging up again.

It just wasn't my time.

"I don't know what *your* plans are," he said, "but *I'm* going to Las Vegas for the weekend." He stood up.

"To do what?"

"Play blackjack. At least it's something I have some control over."

"How do you figure you have any control over *chance*?" I said.

"Better odds," he said. "The odds are better in Las Vegas than they are here."

I was back to my anger.

"Go, then! Maybe you'll meet somebody!"

That's what part of me really wanted. I wanted something to happen to take the heat off me.

"I've considered that," Sandy said, "but I just don't have the energy."

He left the room.

While Sandy was in Las Vegas, I had a super-king-size anxiety attack that even Valium every couple of hours couldn't fix. I had feelings of impending doom, as if the end of the planet earth was at hand.

Only gin could touch that.

When Sandy returned late Sunday afternoon, he looked like a broken man.

"Did you lose a lot?" I asked.

"I won $400."

"That doesn't sound like bad news to me," I said, genuinely puzzled.

"You don't understand. Blackjack is all I've got left. I thought I could do so much better. Now I don't even have *that*!"

And he began to cry.

Never—not once, not even when his patient shot himself—had I seen Sandy off the wall and not make sense. Good old solid Sandy. Fair-play Sandy. Sensible Sandy. Rational Sandy. In-control Sandy. In-command Sandy.

Here he was, hunched over the kitchen table and weeping like a little child because he'd won "only $400."

That's when I saw the whole situation very, very clearly:

I was fine. It was *Sandy* who was crazy.

# – 14 –

# ESKIMO

*We cannot leave the trap until we know we are in it.*
    *—Marilyn Ferguson*
    The Aquarian Conspiracy

My mother flew out from Connecticut to see the children and, I think, to check up on me. She was upset about my thinness.

"Justine said you were thin, but this is terrible!" she said, poking at my clavicle bone.

"I do a lot of bike riding," I explained.

She was relentless. Daily, she cornered me with questions about Emily and daily I did what I could to skate away from them.

"All a child needs is love," she kept saying, "especially a troubled child like Emily."

That one really zinged me. Love was the one thing I didn't think I was capable of. After all, I couldn't feel it—not for Sandy, not for my children, not for my mother. I just felt—nothing. Guilt, maybe, but not anything else.

Where had my love feelings gone?

"I have work to do," I said.

"You're trying to save the world and you can't even save yourself," she said.

For two whole weeks my mother sat in the garden with her adoring granddaughters on her lap. She must have read them a hundred stories. She took walks with them, played giggly games with them, colored with them, sang to them. She was wonderful to them.

83

But I didn't want to read stories and giggle around with children. I used to be afraid if I started it, they'd capture me over to their side and I'd be stuck there.

And then I couldn't do my work.

On lovely days I closed myself in my dark little office like a mole and worked until the sun set. I'd just sold a book proposal called "The Feminist's Handbook" to a major New York publisher. It was to be a kind of introduction to the women's movement and probably would have been one of the first to appear. But even though I'd signed the contract and accepted the advance money, somehow I knew that this book would never be born.

"You're no fun anymore," Sandy said. "You never want to go anywhere. You hate parties. You think movies are irrelevant. What the hell else is there to do? I don't understand why you can't just be happy."

"I could be happy if you'd get more involved with NOW. Then we could do things together."

"How about showing a little interest in what I do? You've never even seen where I work and I've been there a year."

"I don't have time. I'm on the go seven days a week!"

"That's your choice."

I was a guest on a late-night radio talk show. I'd had two martinis before leaving the house. It had taken all my self-control not to have more.

During a commercial break, despite the breath mints, the talk show host asked me if I'd been drinking.

Never had anybody except Sandy asked me such a question directly.

"Do I sound funny?"

"Not really," he said. "But I can smell it. Better have some coffee."

I felt humiliated.

When I got home Sandy was waiting up for me with a bottle of champagne. "Good job!"

I was delighted with the champagne. I was dying for a drink and that gave me permission to do it openly.

I wanted so badly to ask him if he could tell I was tight that first hour on the air, but I didn't dare. I didn't want to rock the boat. A glass of champagne in peace was more important.

The day after my mother flew back to Connecticut, I let myself think about some of the things she said were worrying her about me: my nervousness, weight loss, sleeping problems.

Once again, I concluded that my problem was that I smoked too much. If I didn't smoke, I'd eat more, drink less, and maybe even sleep better.

I'd read about a stop-smoking clinic in Sherman Oaks, so I called and made an appointment.

Immediately I felt better. At least I was doing something about my life.

*The Eskimo Story:*
*These two men, one an atheist and the other a religious man, were having a drink at a bar in Alaska. The conversation turned to God. "I don't believe in your God," said the atheist. "No? Why not?" said the religious man. "Because," said the atheist, "I gave him a chance to prove himself to me once and he didn't come through." "Tell me what happened," said the religious man. "Well, I was stranded in a blizzard," said the atheist, "and I got down on my knees and prayed, 'God, if you're there, save me now!'" "But, you're* here—*so God must exist." "Hell, no!" said the atheist. "Some Eskimo came along and led me back to civilization."*

In my life, Harlan Yates was an Eskimo. Harlan Yates was my counselor at the smoking clinic. Blond, handsome and thirty, I got a crush on him in five minutes.

His office was small and comfortable with personal touches—a guitar leaning against the wall, a peace poster, photos of his small twin daughters, and assorted knickknacks.

Unlike Sandy, Harlan loved to talk—not just about ideas but about feelings.

Talking about feelings was a new experience for me. Whenever I'd been in therapy, I'd talk about thinking but not about how I felt. I didn't even know that thinking and feeling are two different things.

"Ever hear of Gestalt therapy?" he asked.

"Yes, but I don't know what it is."

"It's about feelings. You ought to consider it. You're a head-tripper. It might help you get out of your head and into your heart. Like what are you feeling right now?"

"Well, I agree with what you're saying—"

Harlan winced. "'Agree' is not a feeling, it's a thought. A feeling is the object of the verb 'to feel'—I feel sad, I feel mad, I feel glad, I feel hurt, I feel sexy—" (my heart jumped when he said this) "—I feel disappointed, I feel afraid. But you can't say, I feel 'agree.' Do you understand?"

"I think so."

"Good. Okay, so what do you feel?"

It was so hard for me to get this. For as long as I could remember I'd ignored what was going on inside my body, the anxiety, the butterflies, the shallow breathing, the racing heart, the nervousness. Thoughts and ideas were what I assumed were important.

"Well," said Harlan, "let's have it."

"I feel like an ass!" I said.

The smoking program involved one-hour sessions three times a week to discuss problems that might trigger smoking and to learn relaxation techniques.

After the first week, Harlan started running overtime.

"Don't worry about it," he said. "Business here is terrible. Nobody wants to stop smoking. I've got nothing but time. Besides," he went on, "I enjoy talking to you and finding out what a male chauvinist pig I am. You'll be happy to know I've stopped sending my laundry home to my mother."

I smiled.

"Aren't you going to ask me who does it now?"

"Who does it now?"

"My ex-wife!" He laughed. I laughed. God, how long it had been since I just simply laughed!

I set about investigating the world of Gestalt therapy. I read some books and even talked Sandy into a Gestalt therapy weekend in the woods of Topanga Canyon. I was there in my high heels and full make-up and Sandy was there in his gray flannel Brooks Brothers slacks. Everybody else was there in sandals and jeans.

We sat on the floor in a circle and I got jumped on for "storytelling" and for being "in my head." Sandy got jumped on for doing what he did so well: not talking.

"I resent you for sitting there on your butt all weekend and not sharing," one of the group said to Sandy. "It feels like you're being judgmental."

After that weekend Sandy refused to have anything further to do with Gestalt therapy.

I, on the other hand, made "getting in touch with feelings" my newest obsession. When Emily's Freudian psychiatrist moved to Houston, I switched her to a Gestalt therapist who had beanbags in her office for Emily to jump into and curl up in.

One early morning I overheard Emily talking to herself in her room as she was struggling to put on a sock that was too small. I heard her start to whimper and then stop herself and say: "How do I feel? How do I feel?" and then when that didn't help she screeched, "MOMMY!!!"

I began to tell Harlan about my marriage, but in so doing was fearful that I was being unfair. I kept assuring Harlan that Sandy had many fine qualities.

"I'm sure he does," said Harlan. "But what I found out in my marriage is that it doesn't matter what fine qualities the other person has, it's are you happy living with them? Is daily life a pleasure? Or is it painful? What's important is what you really feel, not what you think you should feel."

I found that statement enlightening—and freeing.

It meant I didn't have to make Sandy the bad guy to justify my being unhappy.

It was just the first step towards my beginning to turn the spotlight on myself.

What I didn't tell Harlan about, of course, was my drinking.

I kept that a secret.

During the last half of each session, Harlan would dim the lights and lead me in a relaxation exercise.

"Today we're going to imagine that you're a non-smoker on a vacation," he said one afternoon. "Now which do you prefer, the ocean or the woods?"

"The woods."

"Fine. Close your eyes and imagine you're in the woods. It's a beautiful day—" ("His voice is beautiful!" was what I was thinking.) "—and it's warm and sunny. There's a soft breeze and as you walk towards your cabin you can smell the flowers and the clean air because you're a non-smoker and your lungs are clear. You enjoy the rich scent of the pine trees and the sweetness of the flowers—gardenias, night-blooming jasmine—"

"Night blooming?" I interrupted. "In the daytime?"

"This is your fantasy, Sylvia," Harlan said patiently. "You can have anything in it you want."

"I want you!" I thought. And I smiled as I remembered the joke about the woman who dreamed a man broke into her bedroom. "What are you going to do with me?" the woman said nervously. "Are you going to kill me? Rob me? Rape me?" and the intruder answered, "It's your dream, madam!"

So, since it was my fantasy, I put Harlan in it. I had him walk with me, talk with me, hold me, kiss me, make love to me and whisper nice things in my ear about feelings.

When we reached the end of the exercise, Harlan turned the lights back up.

"Well, how was it?" he said. "Relaxing, huh?"

"Very nice," I said.

"Now I want you to start doing that on your own, every day."

And I did. I thought about Harlan every day.

Looking back on it, I know Harlan Yates saved my life. He didn't mean to. He was just "doing his thing," but because he put me "in touch with my feelings" he forced me to see that I was miserable.

And pain is the first step towards healing.

That afternoon as I drove home to from the valley, I turned east towards Cheviot Hills instead of west towards Brentwood. I ended up on Veda's doorstep, ringing her doorbell.

The minute I was inside, without even asking me, Veda went to her bar and made me a martini.

Then she made herself a Scotch.

I got right to the point.

"Veda, when you were married to Lloyd, did you ever have an affair?"

Veda looked at me with her wide, black eyes and laughed. "My lord!" she said. "Do you mean you haven't?"

Officially I was now an ex-smoker. I went back to see Harlan for my last session.

I was sad. I'd never see him again and I wanted to see him again.

"Harlan," I said. I was feeling nervous! "I'm about to take a risk, so don't interrupt me. I like you a lot. Will you go out with me?"

By now I was shaking. I'd just propositioned a man for the first time in my life. And I was married!

Harlan didn't flinch or even miss a beat. "I was hoping you'd do that," he said. "How about my house tonight around 7:30?"

That was it.

Harlan came around the desk, leaned over my chair and gently embraced me. Then, kissing me on both cheeks European style, he said:

"I hate to ask you such a mundane question, but won't your husband notice you're missing?"

"He works late on Thursdays," I said.

Five o'clock came and went and I didn't drink or take more than half a Valium. I knew I couldn't drink and commit adultery at the same time and tonight my priority was adultery.

Adultery—what a powerful word!

The word alone was almost enough to stop the deed—but it was too late. I was beyond that now. Without quite knowing why, I knew this thing was a stepping stone towards saving my own life.

There was no logic to that—it was just a feeling.

I found Harlan's little house in Laurel Canyon. He greeted me in cut-off jeans and a sweatshirt. His furnishings consisted of a mattress on the living room floor, a bicycle in the corner, bookcases made of boards and cinder blocks, a chair, a stereo, and a color TV.

"I bought the television on my birthday," he said. "I figured if I was going to be in the over-thirty generation I should have something materialistic to show for it."

I sat down on the mattress and took off my heels.

"The steaks are on. Want some wine? It's only Ripple."

I'd never heard of Ripple.

"No thanks," I said.

"Grass?"

"No thanks."

He picked up his guitar, the one from the office, and played along with Creedence Clearwater. It was all so—hippy. I loved it.

We ate.

Harlan drank a lot of Ripple. "Sometimes I think I'm on my way to being an alcoholic."

I laughed.

I knew he was just kidding.

Then he offered me some white powder.

"What is that?"

"Cocaine."

"Isn't that what Freud used?" I'd read about that in graduate school.

Harlan laughed. "You're a real babe in the woods, aren't you! You surprise me."

I wasn't tempted by the cocaine. I had little curiosity about drugs. I took Valium, Dexedrine, Ritalin, Nembutal, Seconal—but they weren't "drugs"—they were "pills."

Then Harlan smoothly seduced me. Since that's what I was there for, I was very cooperative. The actual act itself was unremarkable, but that wasn't important. Doing it and getting to the other side of it was what was important to me.

We lay there naked on his mattress.

"Want a blanket?" he asked.

I nodded. It was getting chilly.

He pulled the blanket up from the end of the bed. He held me. "I didn't think you'd be so intense," he said.

I wasn't sure if I'd just been complimented or insulted. But what I did know was that I reacted with a feeling—fear.

"I'll have to go soon," I said.

Harlan didn't try to talk me out of it.

"Is something wrong?" I asked.

"I'm feeling a little out of it. I guess it's the steak."

We lay there silently for a while longer and then I crawled out and got dressed. Harlan put on his cut-offs.

At the door he gave me a kiss on the cheek. "I'll call you tomorrow from work," he said.

I was flooded with relief. At least I'd have something to look forward to.

When I got home I took a shower to wash off my sin, astonished at how good I felt. I'd expected to feel guilty, but instead I felt victorious and strong—which at first I assumed had something to do with my getting rid of my dreary New England puritan sex hang-ups.

But it was more than that.

Having committed adultery, I was now free to move on.

# – 15 –

# BLOWS

*If ten Indians tell you you're drunk, you'd better lie down.*
*—Indian wisdom*

"Sorry to call so late," Harlan said to me on the phone the next afternoon. It was almost time for Sandy to be getting home and I'd been waiting on tenterhooks for this call. "Believe it or not, we were *busy* today and I wanted to wait until I had time to talk without being rushed."

Inside I was getting another *feeling*—a kind of "oh-oh, he's leading up to something" feeling.

I was right.

"I've been thinking," Harlan said. "I think we made a mistake. I thought I could handle it, but you seem so needy, so intense—" (So that's what he'd meant by that word last night!) "—and I'm just not in a place where I can handle being involved. I want something casual. You don't seem like a woman who can just be casual."

"What did I *do?*" I said, starting to cry.

"You didn't *do* anything. It doesn't even have anything to do with your being married. I knew you were married. It's something else that's going on with you that I can't put my finger on, but whatever it is I know I can't handle it."

Immediately what popped into my head was "gin."

But how could Harlan know about that?

Harlan kept right on talking. "It's my fault for coming on to you. I like you. You attract me. I didn't think it through and I'm sorry. I just thought I should tell you right away before you start to care."

*Start* to care!

"Do you understand?" he added.

I didn't.

He was talking about consequences, and considering consequences of actions wasn't even in my frame of reference. I wanted Harlan *now* and I'd worry about consequences later. Why couldn't he do that?

It was like he read my mind: "I mean what I'm saying, Sylvia, even if you don't understand."

"I know." I *did* know.

"I'll call you in a week to see how you're doing," he said kindly.

"Okay," I said. At least that was something.

"Don't forget your relaxation exercises. You have to keep them up, it's important."

"Okay," I said.

"Goodbye."

"Goodbye."

As soon as I hung up, I went into the kitchen, got a pack of cigarettes out of the drawer, took one out of the pack and lit it.

I'd kept my months of preoccupation with Harlan a secret from Sandy. I'd kept my infidelity a secret from Sandy. But I couldn't keep Harlan's rejection a secret. I was so hurt it showed all over.

I confessed.

And to my astonishment, Sandy's reaction to my confession of adultery was a shrug.

A shrug!

He wasn't even going to fight for me!

We made a last-ditch effort to "save the marriage" by going to see a marriage counselor. I heard myself saying that if Sandy would only do A or stop doing B or change C—*then* everything would be okay. But I knew better. I was only paying lip service to patching things up. I knew that even if Sandy changed from an apple into an orange, I still wasn't going to be happy.

It was beating a dead horse and the psychologist, who was busy "relating upward" because Sandy was a psychiatrist, missed it completely.

We stopped couple therapy.

My infidelity had only been mentioned once in passing. It had no impact on the therapist either.

The subject of my drinking hadn't even come up.

A few months before the end, Sandy and I went to a cocktail party. Usually I made Sandy go places by himself so I could stay home and have my own party the way I liked it—alone.

At one point during the evening I found myself, martini in hand, sitting next to a woman who had no drink in sight. When I took a gulp, she watched me. Very strange, I thought. I didn't like it at all.

"Aren't you having anything?" I asked her.

"No. I don't drink," she said simply.

I waited for some sort of explanation—on a diet or something—but there was none.

So I launched into self-defense: "I had a *day* today like you wouldn't believe!" I said. "This is the first moment I've had a chance to relax!"

She smiled.

"Are you sure I can't get you something?" I asked. It was really making me nervous that she was sitting there doing nothing.

"I'm fine. I don't drink because I'm an alcoholic. I'm in Alcoholics Anonymous." She said this so matter of factly that it caught me off-guard.

"Well, you're probably smart! I'm sure it's bad for the body and too many calories besides!"

"I haven't had a drink in eleven years."

"Good for you!" I gushed. "Do you work?" I added, trying to move on to another topic.

"I'm an actress. I do character parts on TV. And I garden."

I considered trying to recruit her for NOW, but thought better of it. I didn't relish the idea of having her hovering around me watching me drink.

"Excuse me, I want to go talk to my husband. I haven't seen him all day."

I edged away over to where Sandy was standing. "Pretend you know me!" I said. "That woman on the couch is following me. I think she disapproves."

"Did you try to recruit her?"

I nodded. Another lie.

Before I went back for a refill, I made sure the Woman of No Drink wasn't looking my way.

"That's it! No more parties!" I said to Sandy on the way home. "They're superficial and boring and I don't want to waste my time on people who are too unsophisticated to have even heard of women's lib!"

93

"Suit yourself," Sandy said.

A minute later, with considerable urgency, I asked Sandy to pull over to the side of the road.

When he stopped, I opened the door, leaned out, and threw up.

Intellectuals are like the proverbial mule: it usually takes something physical to get their attention.

In my case it took a black eye and a bloody facial cut.

Sandy and I were sitting in the bedroom one evening. It was late— nearly midnight. I'd just come back from a NOW meeting. I was on the loveseat, drink in hand. Sandy was stretched out on the bed in his robe, reading *Time* magazine.

"Your eyes are half-mast again," he said, "which is not the same as saying you have bedroom eyes." He was angry.

"I'm hurting."

"You're always hurting."

"I'm hurting about Harlan." I dabbed at my tearing eyes with a Kleenex.

"You'll get over it."

"You don't even give a damn!"

"Not about that."

"I want to talk about it."

"It's useless talking with you when you're drunk. You never re- member it the next day anyhow."

"You just want to avoid talking about feelings! And you want me to squash down all mine!"

Suddenly I was enraged. That's how my anger came these days— suddenly, volcanically.

I leapt up and flew across the room and threw my Kleenex in Sandy's face.

Sandy, not knowing what I was throwing, swung out to defend himself. He caught my shoulder which sent me spinning sideways towards the bureau. I fell face down into a tray full of perfume bottles before landing on my back on the floor.

My face hurt. When I felt it, it was wet. I looked at my hands—red. Blood! When I felt my hair, it was soaking with blood, too. I started to scream: "I hate you! I hate you!" The more I screamed the more I got into it: "I HATE YOU! I HATE YOU!!"

"Mommy?"

I heard Abby's voice. I'd forgotten all about the children and now they were both standing there in the doorway. "Mommy?" Emily was behind her little sister, chewing on her fingers. They started towards me.

"Sandy, get them out of here!" I screamed. I put my hands over my face so they wouldn't see the blood. "GET THEM OUT OF HERE!" Sandy, still in shock, obeyed like an automaton.

When he came back, I was still lying on the floor, quiet now. The screaming had all gone out of me. He came over and examined me. "There's a cut on the bridge of your nose. It's pretty deep. It'll have to be stitched up. I'll call Dr. Ferris and go tell Mrs. Owens." He was being very calm now, very doctor-like. "Can you get up?"

I nodded and stood up. Sandy helped me into the bathroom. "Are you dizzy?"

I shook my head.

"Good. You've lost a bit of blood, though."

He turned on the shower. "Try to get cleaned up while I make those calls."

When he came back, he told me we were going to the hospital, to the emergency room.

"Emergency room?" I said. I'd never been to an emergency room in my life. Emergency rooms are for…for…other people. Not for *me*.

I wanted to go to my doctor's office.

"It's too late at night for that," Sandy kept trying to explain to me. "He's not there. He's the one who told us to go to emergency."

I felt humiliated. All the way to the hospital I worried about what the emergency room staff was going to think.

"Are you going to tell them that I was drinking?" I asked Sandy.

"I don't think I'll have to."

"They'll probably think it was just a common, ordinary drunken brawl," I said. "They'll put our names down in some file and they'll be there forever!"

Sandy smiled one of his cynical, tired little smiles: "Tell me," he said, "if this wasn't a common, ordinary drunken brawl, just what the hell do you think it *was*?"

"It was an accident!"

"When are you going to start telling the truth?"

I looked gruesome. I had a patch over one eye and my nose was bandaged and I had a bump on my forehead.

In the kitchen next morning Abby was fascinated by my bandages. She kept trying to touch them. Emily, as usual, wasn't paying attention. She was marching to her own little drummer, checking out the crumbs in the cracks of the kitchen table.

Sandy was reading the paper.

I tried to explain it all to Abby. "Mommy had an accident and hurt herself."

"Mommy and Daddy were fighting," Abby said.

"Yes, but Daddy didn't mean to hurt Mommy. It was an accident."

Suddenly Sandy got up and left the room.

I stood up to follow. Abby suddenly panicked and clung to me. "I want to go!"

" No, you stay here with Emily and Mrs. Owens. I'll be right back." I raced after Sandy and followed him up the stairs and into the bedroom.

Sandy sat down on the loveseat, bent over and put his face in his hands.

"What is it?" I said, alarmed.

When he looked up, there were tears streaming down his face.

"Every time I look at you I feel sick inside," he said. "I'm so sorry. God, I'm sorry!" He uttered a deep, agonized wail. For a second I felt a quickening in my heart. Was it a feeling for him? Was it caring?

I sat down on the edge of the bed, frozen as Sandy spoke, his face contorted with pain. God, could men feel this kind of pain? I thought they were immune. "I've been feeling so helpless," he said. "I kept trying to figure out if I was to blame for your drinking—that you must be doing it for some reason. I kept thinking I could find some way of making you not want to drink—but I didn't want to hurt you! I didn't mean to hurt you!"

I couldn't bear it. I couldn't deal with it. What about *my* pain? How could I pay attention to Sandy's pain when I had so much of my own?

I knew this was a moment of decision. I knew what I should do if I wanted to save us: I should get up and go over to him, comfort him, put my arms around him, hold him and let him know it wasn't his fault. My insides screamed: Take responsibility, Sylvia! He's offering you another chance to see into his soul—just as he did that night in Boston a million years ago when his patient blew his brains out.

But this time I wasn't up to it. This time I was rooted to the spot, frozen, immobilized.

I let the moment pass. The choice was made—and we both knew it.

I went cold inside. I no longer cared one way or the other what Sandy was feeling.

The marriage was over.

# – 16 –

# FALL-APART

*We have to lose our minds in order to come to our senses.*
                                                    —*Fritz Perls*

My real father fell apart in a sanatorium in Westport, Connecticut. My stepfather fell apart at home surrounded by his books on mental health. And I fell apart in the luxurious Hotel Bel Air Sands, nestled up against the Santa Monica mountains in Brentwood, California.

It was only a mile away from the house.

I told Sandy I was checking in to "think things out."

I knew I was never coming back again.

I left the big house, the pool, the kids, the cats, the bougainvillea, the birds of paradise, the fountain, the fireplaces, the poolman, the gardener, the maid, the nurse. I left behind what Zorba the Greek called "the whole catastrophe"—and I moved into a hotel room.

I brought with me only the most important items: I brought my typewriter (I still planned to write my book and I had the go-ahead from a men's magazine to write an article called "What Women's Liberation Will Do for Men"!). I brought my makeup. And I brought two bottles of gin, one bottle of vermouth—and some clothes.

Once I'd put my belongings away, I didn't know what to do with myself. It was only one o'clock in the afternoon. I turned on the TV, flipped the channels, and turned it off again.

I felt an anxiety attack coming on and this one was a lulu. I pictured myself as a glass vase about to explode from a force so strong that the pieces of me would go off in all directions and sail out windows.

I kept wishing I could call room service and have them send a bellhop upstairs to my room to hold onto me so I wouldn't shatter. But even I could tell that it was inappropriate and might be misunderstood.

It was too early to drink. I was too late to write. I was too upset to read. The girls were still in school and didn't even know yet that I'd left them. Mrs. Owens and Sandy would have to pick up *those* pieces.

I called my Gestalt therapist (I'd started individual treatment) and begged for an emergency appointment. When Jane said yes, it was like a reprieve. I raced to Beverly Hills, even though I was an hour and a half early. I felt safer there in the little waiting room than I did alone in the hotel.

When Jane called me in, I threw myself in the middle of her large beanbag (she had one too) and curled up in a fetal position.

I was so happy to be there.

"I left Sandy today," I said.

"Ah-hah. No wonder." Jane studied me a minute. "How do you feel?"

Shades of Harlan!

"I feel anxious. I feel scared. I feel guilty. I feel angry. I feel excited. I feel relieved."

"How about hungry? Your thinness concerns me. Here, eat some of these."

She tossed me a little box of Sunmaid raisins.

"I can't," I said.

"I know, but I want you to do it anyway. Eat some raisins and tell me what you're experiencing as you're doing it. It's an experiment."

I put a few raisins on my tongue—and gagged.

"What were you *feeling* just then when you gagged, Sylvia?"

"—that I can't stomach my life!" I said. "Jane!" I called out her name with such intensity it surprised me.

"What?" she said, alarmed herself.

"I've been drinking!"

She didn't fall through the floor.

"You have a choice about that, you know," she said, making it sound like no big deal. "You can choose to drink or you can choose not to drink."

My heart sank. She didn't understand. Gestalt therapists were always talking about choice and it sounded great, but I knew I couldn't do it. When it came to gin I drank against my will. I had no choice.

I knew then that I wouldn't be able to discuss this with Jane anymore. I could talk to her about anything else, but not this. When it came to gin, she was one of "them."

"I want you to try another experiment," she said later. "I went to this conference on megavitamin therapy and it might help you. I want you to start taking high doses of vitamin C and Niacinamide, 3000 mgs. of each three times a day. Will you do that?"

"What's it for?" I asked.

"It's supposed to be very helpful for schizophrenics, alcoholics and ruminators."

I thought about that for a minute. What did that have to do with *me*? I knew I wasn't a schizophrenic, so that wasn't it. And even though I'd mentioned drinking, we most certainly weren't talking about *alcoholism* here, so *that* wasn't it. That left "ruminators"—people who think too much.

Jane obviously wants me to take vitamins, I concluded, because she thinks I think too much. Or in Harlan's words, "because you're a head-tripper."

"Okay," I said.

I bought the vitamins on the way back to the hotel.

Back in my room, I hurriedly splashed gin over ice cubes (it was now past five o'clock) and used it to wash down the vitamin C and Niacinamide. I turned on the TV and lay down on the bed and watched a rerun of "Bachelor Father." I kept thinking of Sandy at home with the girls. I wondered if they missed me, if they were hurting because I'd left them. The idea was so painful that I got up and made another drink.

Like Scarlett O'Hara, I'd have to think about all that tomorrow.

The next afternoon when I knew Sandy was at work and Mrs. Owens had gone to pick up the children at school, I snuck back to the house for more clothes—and some more gin.

When I walked into the kitchen there were children's blocks all over the kitchen floor. I stood there intending to pick them up but suddenly my brain just seemed to quit functioning. It snapped.

I couldn't figure out how to pick up little wooden blocks off the kitchen floor! I stood there and didn't know what to do. I felt overwhelmed.

Finally, I figured out that by making myself focus on one block at a time, the one right at my feet, I could tune out all the other blocks and then the task seemed a little less overwhelming.

101

I faced Block 1. I bent down. I reached for it. I put my hand on it. I lifted it. I stood up. I walked like a robot to the toy box. I dropped Block 1 into the toy box. Clunk. I turned and faced Block 2. I repeated the steps I'd just taken on Block 1 for Block 2. Then Block 3. I repeated this process for Blocks 4, 5, 6, 7—and after a few minutes I began to get the hang of it. I started to go faster. I was less jerky, and finally it was as though I became unstuck.

The job was done.

I felt exhausted. I sat down at the kitchen table. "That was a close call!" I said to myself. It felt as though I'd just pulled myself back from the edge of a precipice. "You almost went out into the Great Void *that* time, Sylvia! Next time you might not get back, just like old Anetta lying catatonic on a bed back at Boston State Hospital."

Every day I drove into Beverly Hills to see Jane. I'd lie in the middle of her beanbag and weep or rage or do whatever I had to do. I just didn't talk about gin.

Strange thing about the gin—I assumed I'd drink less once I was away from Sandy—no more fights and upsets.

Instead, the drinking was worse.

It was truly puzzling.

I liked the way Jane did therapy. She didn't go for that "blank screen" approach where the therapist says nothing and the patient does all the talking—the way I'd been trained. Instead, she shared. She told me things about herself, even her imperfections and mistakes. She told me about a relationship she was in that wasn't going well. She showed me it was okay to be a human being.

So long as I was trying to maintain an image of "perfect," I couldn't admit I had a drinking problem. Perfect people don't have drinking problems. So even though Jane and I weren't really discussing gin, she was helping me chip away at my defenses and get closer to the Truth.

In addition to emoting in Jane's office, at least once a week I drove high up into the mountains of Topanga Canyon to the Topanga Center for Human Development for Gestalt groups. Again and again, I'd throw myself into the center of a ring of people, like some kind of sacrifice and "work." Often the group facilitator didn't have much experience, but it didn't matter. I found tremendous relief there, just as my grandfather, decades earlier, had found relief on that couch from Bloomingdale's, unloading his soul to a psychoanalyst who didn't even understand English.

This was how I began to learn that it's patients, not therapists, who do the healing.

The only thing that remained untouched was my drinking.

After two-and-a-half weeks at the Hotel Bel Air Sands, I found a one-room "pad" on the Marina del Rey peninsula and rented it. I traded in my new black Chrysler station wagon for a second-hand Mustang convertible. I drove to the house one summer evening to break the news to Sandy that I wasn't coming home.

The girls were in the driveway and didn't recognize my car. I was like a stranger driving up. When I got out they ran over and hugged me.

"Take me for a ride," Abby said. Her penchant for travel started early.

"Someday," I said.

"Someday" was my answer for everything.

Sandy came over to look at the car. "What did you do with the station wagon?"

"I traded it in."

"What did you get for it?"

"*This*." I tapped on the Mustang.

"You were taken," he said simply.

"I don't care. I'm changing my image." I gave a little nervous laugh. I didn't want to have a station wagon. Housewives have station wagons.

Sandy and I went over and sat by the pool.

"I'm not coming back," I said.

"I thought you were just going to the hotel to think things out."

"I did," I said, lying. "And now I've decided I'm not coming back."

"Have it your way," Sandy said. And then he did it again! He shrugged!

"Is that all you've got to say when I tell you I'm leaving you?"

"What do you want me to say?"

"What do you *feel*?!" I said, raising my voice.

"Right now I feel I hate your guts," he said.

I got up. "Oh, go to hell!"

I drove off without even saying goodbye to the girls, but I could see them in my rearview mirror, waving to me as I drove down the long gravel driveway.

It was a picture that imprinted itself on my mind and I couldn't get rid of it.

Not even gin made that one disappear.

# – 17 –

# DOOR SLAMMING

*I do my thing and*
*You do your thing.*
*If we find each other,*
*It's beautiful.*
*If not,*
*It can't be helped.*
        *—Fritz Perls*
        *Gestalt prayer*


*Do your thing and I shall know you.*
        *—Ralph Waldo Emerson*

The first time I heard the Gestalt prayer I cried.

It relieved some of my guilt about leaving Sandy and the children.

When Nora in Ibsen's play, *A Doll's House*, slammed the door on her marriage, the sky fell in. I guess in some ways that's what I was expecting would happen to me. But what I quickly discovered was that times had changed.

By 1970 the women's movement had finally hit the front pages. We became legitimized, even glamorized. Suddenly it became chic for a woman to run away from home to "find herself" and "do her thing." All over American Noras began slamming doors. I was one of them.

Instead of slings and arrows I got pats on the back for my courage, my guts.

Now if Sandy had been the one to walk out on me first it would have been different—especially if I'd ended up with the house, the kids and the "things." That would have been embarrassingly old-fashioned. But because I was the one to "do a Nora" and leave, I acquired a kind of status: Liberated Woman.

So there I was, alone in a tiny one-room "pad" in the Marina with one of the two family cats, holding up the banner for independence and still, much to my surprise, drinking myself into oblivion.

In light of the emotional support from friends, I was surprised to receive a form letter from the Los Angeles County Conciliation Court offering Sandy and me an appointment with a licensed marriage counselor to see if they could help us "save" our marriage.

Save our marriage! I was furious! Was this some kind of male chauvinist plot to keep me tied to hearth and home? How *dare* the county interfere with my quest for liberation?

I took these things personally.

On August 26, 1970, I took part in a demonstration to celebrate the fiftieth anniversary of women's suffrage.

It was to be my swan song in NOW.

Betty Friedan declared that August 26 would be a national "Women's Strike Day" and made a plea for women everywhere to refuse to go to work to protest the fact that while we had the vote, we didn't have much else. NOW had organized demonstrations in many major cities, including Los Angeles.

I dressed to the teeth in a shocking pink crepe dress, matching scarf and pink tinted sunglasses. (On my death bed I'd still insist on being color-coordinated!) I spent a long time on my make-up. These days I *had* to because most mornings I was so shaky from being hung over (I still thought it was "nerves") that I had to apply make-up by bracing my elbow against the bathroom mirror just to steady my hand. And as a finishing touch to my outfit, I took my collection of nearly fifty women's lib protest buttons and pinned them all up and down the front of my pink dress.

I made such a good "visual" that I ended up on the front page of the *San Francisco Chronicle* the next morning, being described in the caption as a "glum feminist."

That night to celebrate what was felt to be a successful day (meaning lots of publicity) we all met at a NOW member's Santa Monica apartment for some food and drink.

I celebrated with drink.

106

I drank until I quietly lay down on the couch and passed out, the party still in full swing. Unlike Atlanta, this time I had no gratuitous warnings, no blessed "Faye's rays" to tell me to get out of there before it was pumpkin time. Nothing. I just went right out in front of the very people whose opinions of me mattered most, including NOW's national president who was in Los Angeles on business.

When I woke up the next morning, still dressed in my shocking pink with the protest buttons sticking into me like a bed of nails, I was humiliated.

Later, some of my NOW associates were eager to let me off the hook by blaming Sandy. "He's such a bastard. This separation has been so hard for you and he's got you all upset—no *wonder*!" one said in my defense.

I nodded, but inside where the truth was hidden and still waiting to see the light, I knew better. I hadn't laid eyes on Sandy in two weeks, so whatever the cause of my August 26 drunk was, *he* wasn't it.

The next day I resigned from women's liberation.

No more NOW, I said. No more meetings. No more demonstrations. No more newsletters. No more press releases. No more media appearances. No more board meetings. No more trips. No more nothing. *Out*!

"There's plenty of new blood in the movement now that we're hot," I said. "And I need time to write my book." I was always ready with reasons.

I intended to write my book, but I didn't.

Instead, I wrote long, personal letters to my agent in New York (who hardly knew me) and told her all about my sufferings. I did a fall-apart for her on paper, talking to her as though she cared.

She didn't.

"I don't earn my ten percent from your letters," she snapped at me in a hurried phone call from Manhattan. "I need to see some chapters of *The Feminist's Handbook* and soon before it's too late. The timing for this is *now*."

I reacted by becoming indignant. I felt pressured. I didn't *like* feeling pressured. Who was *she* to pressure me like that, especially after all I was going through.

Well, to hell with her! I said. To hell with her and the publisher and the book too. Who needs it!

I wrote her another letter and backed out of the book—as though it had no value. I threw away the one thing that might have made the difference in the writing career I said I wanted—chucked it without a thought for possible consequences or regrets.

Instead I congratulated myself on my new and superior values. Today I was focused on the here and now instead of being hung up on superficial things like having a book published, creative success, and financial gain. Big deal! It didn't occur to me that being independent meant being able to *pay* for it!

The breaking of my contract had limited impact on my agent. She simply handed the whole mess over to a lawyer and washed her hands of me.

Without knowing that I was doing it, I'd managed to eliminate from my life just about everything that was in it—my marriage, my kids, my home, my things, my car, my social life, my health, my "cause," and now my work.

I had nothing left.

Except an empty life. A void.

Yet I had no conscious sense of loss. I was numb to it. I was "doing my thing" and "finding my space" and letting the chips fall where they may.

When I didn't have my book to write, I returned to writing letters. I typed a ten-page, single-spaced letter to Harlan all about my feelings. I was sure he'd be fascinated. After all, he was the one who introduced me to them.

By return mail I got my own letter back with a note scribbled across the top: "Sorry, Sylvia, but I just can't get into this. Harlan."

That one hit me hard. I cried over it. And, of course, I drank over it.

At night I either drank myself into oblivion ("falling asleep early" I was still calling it) or I didn't drink (which was hard) and drove up the winding mountain road to Topanga Center so I could emote in Gestalt encounter groups. I could "let it all hang out" there—all except anything that had to do with gin.

I also went up to Topanga to meet men—men like Harlan who were "into feelings,"—not to mention men who were into breaking up their marriages, just as I was.

Until my Topanga summer, I'd only made love to my two husbands and to Harlan—once.

My next step was to change that.

108

I met Barney at one of the regular Friday night drop-in encounters. He was a flight instructor for a little local airport. He had deep brown cow-like eyes that made my heart melt and that night when I was busy "working" on my guilt in the center of the Gestalt circle, a part of me was conscious that Barney was watching me.

At one point the group facilitator threw a pillow into the middle of the ring and said: "Okay, Sylvia, pretend that pillow is Sandy and tell him how guilty you feel about leaving him."

I got right into it: "Sandy, I feel so guilty about leaving you. I feel like I've ruined your life. I feel responsible for your feelings. But I was dying inside, Sandy, and I had to go out and *find* myself. But I still feel like I'm such a terrible person—"

"—Why don't you check that feeling out with some of the people in this room," the group leader interrupted. "See if people here think you're a terrible person."

"I imagine they do," I said meekly.

"Check it out! Don't mindfuck about it! *Ask* them!"

"I'm scared," I said.

"Tough!" he said. "Let's see if you have any guts."

That got to me. Of course I had guts. That was my *thing*!

God, I loved this stuff! I loved pushing at my feelings, right to the limit—"pushing into the red zone" as one of my Gestalt trainers used to call it. I loved the dangerously thrilling prospect of confronting someone in the safety of a group like this and not knowing what they might say or what I might feel as a result.

I crawled across the carpet and stopped in front of Barney, my heart pounding.

"You have the warmest eyes," I said to him.

"Thanks," he said. "And I think you have a lot of strength."

And that's when I fell in love with him. He thought I was strong.

I moved on to the woman next to him.

"I envy you," she said. "I wish I'd had the guts to do what you did. I was too chicken. I was afraid to leave all that security so I made *him* leave. Now I feel like I was a coward. I think you're marvelous!"

And I thought it was marvelous hearing all this stuff about how tough I was. It was better than being told I was beautiful. One man said: "I think you're the most beautiful woman I've ever seen in person."

"Thank you," I said, but I suspected him of being chauvinistic.

"Beautiful" was a pre-revolutionary compliment.

On a tour over Los Angeles in the Cessna 150, Barney and I flew low over the Brentwood house so I could show it all to him. We could see Mrs. Owens in her white uniform out by the pool with the kids. Barney was impressed.

"You idiot! What did you give all that up for?"

I gave him a little Mona Lisa smile. Now *that* was the kind of compliment I liked!

I was so used to being the one with problems that it never occurred to me that other people had problems, too—that others who spend hours spilling their guts out in Gestalt encounter groups had something wrong with them. I just assumed they had their act together and I was the only one playing catch-up.

Barney's main problem turned out to be money. He was always broke. And because of that I fell into my first "deal." I helped Barney out financially (motorcycle insurance, car repairs, chess set, plus a ten-day vacation for the two of us in Mexico City) and in exchange Barney had to give up his right to bug me about my drinking.

Tit for tat.

Once he said, "Boy, you really down that stuff," but the glare I gave him shut him up fast.

Another time he said to me, lightly, "Guess what? You fell asleep when we were making love last night. I guess you were pretty tired, right?"

I thought: Oh, God, here's the same conversation I had with Sandy all over again!

But since Barney had just handed me my excuse, I went for it. "Yes," I said. "I was beat."

I wasn't even faithful to him.

I was "liberated" now. Marriage or even being exclusive with somebody meant you weren't liberated, so I couldn't do that. I didn't want to be tied down and suffocated with chauvinistic demands.

"Look Ma, No Guilt!" I said in letters home to my mother describing my new, free life.

"It all sounds so *hectic*," she wrote back. "Are you sure you're okay?"

Six months after I'd walked out on Sandy, Mrs. Owens did the same. She quit.

"I'm not happy here in California any more," she said to me. "Since you left, the house is cold and lonely. The girls miss you so and some

110

nights I hear Sandy crying in his room and I can't stand it. I want to go home to Boston and see my sisters."

I had no choice but to agree to take Emily and Abby and find a new place to live. The idea was very scary.

"I worry about you, Sylvia," Mrs. Owens said to me on the way to the airport. "You're still so thin. And you mustn't try to handle things with drinking. It's not good for you."

I wasn't prepared for her to mention drinking. I didn't *like* anyone mentioning drinking.

"Oh, don't worry," I said, "I'm feeling *so* much better and once the girls are with me I'll be too busy to sit around and drink."

"I'm glad to hear you say that." She seemed genuinely relieved. Emily and Abby were like granddaughters to her.

Having been a part-time mother at best, I took on my own two children full-time. They were four and six—and they were strangers. I didn't know the first thing about their day-to-day lives.

"When is your bedtime?" I found myself asking them the first night we all moved in to our new little three bedroom apartment in a two-family house on the Playa Del Rey beach.

Later I asked Emily: "What do you wear to school?"

Emily didn't answer. She was in outer space somewhere, so I asked Abby: "Abby, what does Emily wear to school?"

"She wears *these*." Abby pulled out a pair of overalls and a shirt from the suitcase and handed them to me. "She likes these because they don't have a bumpy part."

Because of Emily's supersensitive skin, she'd go into a tantrum if there was a seam in her clothes she could feel.

"What about shoes?" I asked Abby.

"She likes these ones." She picked up some ratty sneakers.

I learned that Abby, at only four, had taken upon her little shoulders the burden of being Emily's caretaker and protector. Wherever Emily went, Abby would follow her with her huge, winsome, hazel eyes—so much like Sandy's—to make sure she didn't disappear, since Emily tended to roam. Abby, though tiny, was proving to be a wise, powerful, and swift little person and I would come to teasingly call her my "willful beast."

Emily wandered around the new apartment with the cat—Emily touching everything twice and the cat sniffing everything. Emily was also naming what she touched, saying it once out loud and once under

111

her breath. "Table [said loud]. Table [said softly]. Picture frame [said loud]. Picture frame [said softly]. Kitchen [said loud]. Kitchen [said softly]."

It drove Abby up the wall.

"Shut up, Emily!" Abby screamed at her.

Emily paid no attention.

"SHUT UP, EMILY!"

"No."

Abby jumped up and gave Emily a shove.

Emily screamed, then cried.

Then they were in a pushing contest with Abby, as usual, winning. Emily was timid and afraid of getting hurt and Abby was reckless and had no fear of anything.

I got nervous. Mrs. Owens, where are you now!

How was I going to handle this?

"Stop it, both of you!" I said.

Neither listened.

I decided to let them kill each other.

I went into the kitchen, unpacked the gin and vermouth, and made a drink.

The next morning I walked into the bathroom and saw towels and little duckies and other bath toys all over the place. Baby shampoo was on the edge of the tub. Apparently I'd given them both a bath last night and shampooed their hair.

I remembered nothing about it.

It flashed through my mind that this was potentially a pretty dangerous situation. One of them could have drowned and I'd have been oblivious to it.

But I didn't know what to do about it.

Emily was in a new school and in first grade. After a week I got that inevitable phone call: "Your child isn't doing too well," the teacher said. "She's in a dream world. I can't seem to get her attention. She doesn't listen. She doesn't seem to understand anything that's going on. Have you ever thought about having her *seen* by somebody?"

"She *is* being seen by somebody."

"Well, let's hope it helps," the teacher said, "because at this rate, she's not going to make it through school."

Why do teachers always call *me*! I said to myself angrily after she'd hung up. Because I'm the mother? Why don't they call Sandy? Why me? Is it *my* fault Emily has a screw loose? After all, Sandy's the one with the schizophrenic aunts! Why don't they pick on him for a change?

I decided that the next time I went to the school, I'd give the teacher Sandy's work phone number so she could interrupt his work day next time instead of mine.

# – 18 –

## GIL

*In the battle between yourself and the world, back the world.*
*—Frank Zappa*

The hardest part about having a drinking problem is pretending you don't have a drinking problem.

That's what I had to do for nearly a year after I met Gil.

Gil was another product of Topanga. He was tall, lean, sensuous and graceful with pale blue eyes that were burned out from smoking so much grass.

Gil was divorced and had custody of his son, Jamie, freeing his ex-wife to go out and do *her* thing—which was hitchhiking around the country with truck drivers.

Jamie was only a month older than Emily. Gil and he lived together in a little hippy house in Venice, just south of Santa Monica. The first time I went to visit, I brought Gil (really *me*) a bottle of wine.

"Thanks, but I don't drink," he said, trying not to let too much of his marijuana smoke escape from his lungs.

After that the trick was to get him to offer me a glass, but I managed.

Gil and Jamie were into the kinds of activities I always avoided— camping, hiking, shell collecting on the beach. But with Gil it was fun so I did it. He absorbed Emily and Abby gladly. I was crazy about him.

I dumped Barney—and Barney reacted badly to being dumped. He took to buzzing my house with his plane. I prayed he had no kamikaze interests he hadn't told me about.

Until Gil, I'd never given much thought to sex. I'd never had an orgasm. Not only that, I didn't care. It was as if all that had no more to do with me than the phone company did. So when Gil started to push at me about sex, I barely comprehended what he was talking about. Here I was enjoying sex with him and he was complaining about it.

"You're holding out on me," he'd say. "I want you to be able to let go."

To me, letting go meant losing control and running amuck. Who'd want to do something like that?

He signed us up for a couple's weekend called "Basic Sensuality." I sat there blushing, almost hiding behind Gil, when the couple running the workshop taught us how to stroke each other by using models of a penis and a vagina. On the second day, couples in the room told us all about their multiple orgasms of the night before.

I'd never felt sexually inadequate until this workshop. I went home in tears.

When Gil wanted us to follow up Basic Sensuality with another weekend called Advanced Sensuality (for this one you had to be willing to take off your clothes—the plaster models wouldn't be used!), I rebelled.

"I don't care if I never come in my whole life, I'm not going to that workshop so forget it!" I screamed at Gil.

"Okay," he said. "But I think you're making a mistake."

He pouted for a few days after that.

Gil got along beautifully with Emily. Being stoned half the time, he was basically a Martian, too, so they understood each other.

One Sunday late afternoon he came over and brought Emily an old goosefeather pillow that had a hole in it just so Emily could go stand on the beach, pull the feathers out and watch them go flying. The four of us went down to the water's edge in front of my house. Gil very formally handed the pillow over to Emily who, as per instructions, reached her little hand in through the hole and pulled out a fistful of feathers and threw them to the wind—and then another and another. Each time she let them go, she jumped up and down happily. Then she chased them as they blew every which way, her long, tangled, dark hair streaming out behind her, her flowered, ankle-length dress billowing around her.

Abby sat primly on the towel next to Gil, Jamie and me, trying to do what she was so used to doing—direct Emily's every move.

116

"*Careful*, Emily! Don't get in the water! Don't throw them *that* way!..."

Gil wouldn't have any of that. "I'll watch her, Abby honey," he said, "so you can just sit here and be a kid, okay?"

"Okay." Abby actually seemed relieved.

Gil wasn't a man I could make deals with about my drinking as I'd been able to do with Barney. Gil made it clear from the starting gate, the first time I drank in front of him, that he didn't like it.

"I'm a pretty tolerant guy, but I can't handle a woman who drinks," he said. "My wife did that so I'm telling you right now—any time you drink too much, no matter where we are, I take Jamie and we go home."

"Everybody drinks now and then," I protested.

"Not around me."

End of discussion.

It looked like I was going to be forced underground.

Neither of us saw smoking grass as a problem, even though Gil did it at the office. He worked as an executive for an airline and he'd never think of going into a business meeting without making a side-trip out to his van in the parking lot for a few hits of weed.

He brought me a ten dollar "lid" of grass as a present. "It's better for you than that rot-gut you drink."

He even gave me lessons: "Take a drag and breathe it way in, way down to your belly button and hold it there."

I did everything he said.

Sometimes I even liked it. It was something to share, to do together.

But as Ogden Nash said, "Liquor is quicker," and since grass took too much time, I preferred liquor. I put Gil's lid on my bureau and it was there for two months, whereas a bottle of gin rarely lasted more than two days. Gin was obviously my drug of choice.

Keeping my drinking hidden from Gil was always easier at his house than at mine. At mine, I was Pavlov's dog—the second I put my key in the front lock, my mouth salivated and I'd head right into the kitchen where I kept the gin. At Gil's house I didn't have this stimulus-response pattern set up so it was better.

Except on nights when it wasn't.

Those were the nights I had to bite the bullet. And after a while I began to cheat.

First there was a drink before I went over to Gil's.

117

From there, I began buying a half-pint of gin on the way and hiding it in my purse. Then I'd sneak into the bathroom for a quick gulp. If he smelled it on my breath, I'd lie and tell him I had "just one" after work.

"Just one, hell, you're drunk," he said to me one night from the bottom of the stairs outside my apartment.

With that he turned and walked off with Jamie scampering after him.

"Please!" I called after him, but I knew it was useless. I knew he'd meant what he'd said.

Gil made me miserable about the drinking. He was the first person to give me a hard time about it and I didn't like it one bit.

But the crazy thing was, I couldn't stop. I wanted the relationship. I knew drinking was the one thing that would drive Gil away. But I couldn't stop.

Obviously, of the two, drinking came first.

When Gil finally did leave me, even though I nearly disintegrated from the pain (being the "leave-*er* was bad enough, but being the "leave-*ee*" was worse), there was still a secret little part of me that said: Whew! Now, at last, I can drink in peace!

Without Gil and without work, I could have jumped head-first into the bottle and stayed there. I could have said, "To hell with waiting for five o'clock—there's nobody watching anymore!"

But I didn't.

A still-functioning survival instinct within me told me to find something to do during the day to keep me off the streets—and within a week of Gil's leaving I wandered, quite literally, into a new career— photography. One day, walking along a street in a neighboring seaside town, I noticed a photography studio. Photography had always been a hobby and all through school I always found myself the unofficial class photographer. I stepped in to look at some prints on display. I stepped out a partner in the business.

Hank was a young, struggling photographer from Texas and this was his first business venture. We made a deal, but this deal had nothing to do with drinking. If I paid half the rent and spent time there, he'd teach me everything he knew and I might even learn enough to begin making money.

Hank was basically a flake, but he did love photography and he also loved his tall wife who had the face of a librarian but the body of a goddess. He never tired of shooting nude pictures of her which *Playboy* kept turning down—not because of her body.

"I'm goin' to try it again usin' that soft-focus technique they're all doin' lately," he'd say. And he'd re-shoot his naked wife using vaseline or a nylon stocking on the lens or a diffusion filter. Then he'd send the pictures back to *Playboy*.

"Persistence is the answer," he'd tell me. "Most people give up too soon."

He kept his word about teaching me photography.

"Now about the lightin'," he said one day, "Keep it *real* simple for those passports. But for portraits, you might could put your first light on the backdrop and your stronger light over here on the client's right side with a fill light on the left—and then you might could shoot at a 60th between 5/6th and an 8th." He paused for a second. "Well, maybe *you* better shoot 125th at 5/6th. I noticed your hand shakes a little bitty too much for a 60th."

I flushed.

I felt exposed—but I don't think Hank even noticed.

The first few times I took passport photos I was a wreck. I was fast becoming a CYA (Cover Your Ass) photographer, taking too many shots and purposely over-exposing everything just to make sure there was something on the negative!

I began to date a Loyola University film student a dozen years my junior who'd taken to hanging around the photography studio. Frank found my drinking "poetic"—a response to the tragedy of my broken romance with Gil. He was so impressed with my drama, in fact, that he starred me in his class project—a half-hour film he wrote about a tragic love affair between an "older woman" (me) and a "much younger man" (he). We shot the movie at my house and on the beach. In the bedroom scene, shot at night (*way* past five o'clock) I was drunk. On film I *looked* drunk. I'd never seen myself drunk and I didn't like it.

Since I ended up editing his film for him in the editing room at Loyola (he was busy studying for finals) I managed to edit out most of the scenes where I looked loaded.

But they made an impression on me.

After a while Frank began to wise up. My drinking became less romantic.

"You know," he commented one time (his eyes all innocence) after I'd polished off nearly a fifth of gin, "your affair with Gil has been over for quite a while. Do you think you're still drinking over that? Or—" he paused, unsure of his ground,"—or do you think maybe you have a *problem?*"

Out of the mouths of babes! I was thinking.

Making my bed one morning soon after this, I had a thunderclap thought: I wasn't *born* drinking gin!

It was the first time I'd noticed "progression." It was the first time I'd looked at my drinking from a distance. What I saw was that my drinking (since I didn't drink gin as a baby) had actually started someplace—Point A (no drinking)—and had progressed to Point B (lots of drinking).

The journey—from Point A to Point B—had taken eight years.

Next thought: Where would I be in another eight years? What would it be like at Point C?

I felt really enlightened by what I'd just seen.

The trouble was, I didn't have the slightest notion what to do about it.

# – 19 –

# GEEK

*Geek (definition): A fool; a sideshow freak in the old circus days whose job it was to stand at the bottom of a pit and eat anything that was thrown in: shoes, chicken heads, broken glass, feces. His payment at the end of the day was a bottle of whiskey. The geek, of course, was an alcoholic.*
— *Paul Rosenberg, M.D.*

A few months after Gil walked out of my life he walked back in.

Only this time he wanted to make a "deal."

His deal was called Open Relationship, a new term then and very "in." Couples gave each other permission to sleep with other people. It was "open and honest" and saved the wear and tear of having to sneak around. Infidelity without cheating.

But we both knew that that wasn't quite what the deal was about. What the deal was really about was drinking. If I was going to drink then Gil was going to be free to see other women; if I was drunk at bedtime I shouldn't be surprised to wake up and find him gone.

By a wild coincidence Gil already had somebody in mind—a Ph.D. named Gudren.

Tit for tat.

I accepted it—which made me a geek and I knew it. But I had entered a new stage of drinking: I *had* to drink. So I had no choice.

And wanting, as always, to be *avant garde* I even defended Open Relationships. "No one person can give another person everything they need," I told Hank's friend Lester from Tennessee.

Lester wasn't having any of it. "That's two-timin' bullshit!" he said. "That son-of-a-bitch would never get away with stuff like that in Nashville!"

Lester was fond of me.

Lester didn't know about the gin.

Gil was experimenting with newer drugs. He'd graduated from grass to hashish. He was still trying to get me off alcohol, but I refused the hashish. The name scared me. It brought to mind Oriental opium dens and sinister people and I wasn't interested.

But LSD was different. When Gil suggested we try it, I was game. LSD brought to mind flower children and peace posters. LSD was *American*.

We drove up into the hills of Topanga Canyon, turned off onto Old Topanga Canyon Road and settled down on a blanket in the middle of a field of tall grass. I even brought along a camera for my "trip." Gil took a plastic baggie out of his shirt pocket. There was a lost-looking little white tablet down in one corner, hardly bigger than a birth-control pill.

"That's *it*?" I said. "That's LSD?" It looked so harmless.

Gil snapped it in half with his pen knife, placed his half on his tongue, closed his mouth and swallowed.

He handed the other half to me.

My heart went ba-BOOM!

I put the LSD in my mouth and swallowed, too. Down it went.

"Now *that*," I said, "is a commitment."

We lay back on the blanket together, holding hands, waiting for the LSD to start working like lovers in a suicide pact.

It was a heavenly day, clear and warm. The sun made me a little sleepy—the long grass swayed hypnotically around us in the breeze. We were surrounded by some serious mountains...they looked so lush, so beautiful...

...I especially enjoyed watching them when they started to breathe. The mountains started rising ever so slowly and then falling, like a woman's chest. It was soothing. Breathe in. Hold. Breathe out. Hold. Breathe in. Hold. Breathe out. Hold. That's it! I thought—the "hold" moment is crucial to understanding the mysteries of life. That's where the answers are, right there in between the breaths—like a crack in the door of the temple.

Focusing carefully on my breathing, at just the right moment, like a surfer, I hitched a ride on my breath so I *was* the breath—I was on the cutting edge of the wave as it unfolded, creating with it the ever-present here and now—each moment being created from the existing moment so that the idea that there are choices in life, "either-or" places, suddenly struck me as a fallacy—there's only the moment, there's only surfing into the next moment from this one...

"Gil?"

"What?"

"I never noticed before that mountains breathe, did you?"

Gil sat up and grinned.

That's when I realized the LSD was already working.

"Wait'll you hear them sing!"

"You mean they don't breathe? It's only the LSD?" I was disappointed.

But on LSD, my "disappointment" wasn't just a feeling, it was the whole world, all there was. I plunged into a black universe of sorrow, terrifying and everlasting, so devastating I thought I would die right there—death from disappointment.

Gil, who'd decided he was there to "trip-sit" me rather than trip out himself, sensed it. "No, mountains really do breathe, it's just that we don't notice it."

Saved!

As fast as I'd plunged into that hell hole of disappointment, I was out again, in ecstasy now, flying, deliriously gleeful, knowing that what I'd seen through the crack in the temple door was real after all—mountains breathe! Oh joy of joys!

"I'm going to take a picture of them breathing!" I announced to Gil. I sat up and reached for my Nikon.

"Lots of luck."

As I fumbled with the camera I used every day, trying to fathom how the damn thing worked, a little girl from one of the nearby houses skipped by. Through the long grass she went, her silky blond hair flying, looking like something out of a children's movie—like Heidi in summer. I forgot about the breathing mountains and aimed my camera at Heidi but by the time I managed to snap, she'd frolicked right out of the frame.

"Damn!" I felt totally helpless.

Gil thought it was all extremely funny. He loved seeing me stoned.

I loved it too.

"When can we do this again?" I said the instant I began to feel it wear off.

"Maybe next week. I think I can get another tab by then."

"*When* next week?" I was really pinning him down.

"I'll let you know."

Because we had our new "deal," I didn't have to sneak drinks when Gil was around any more. And as promised, when I overdid it, he'd leave.

One morning I woke up hung over, expecting that he'd be gone—but he was still there.

Only he was different.

I couldn't quite put my finger on it, but he was just—different.

"What's the matter?" I asked.

"Nothing."

He went off to work.

That night he came back with a fresh lid of grass.

He was still in that strange place.

When the girls were in bed and Jamie had crashed on the couch, we walked down to the edge of the ocean and sat down on our towels. It was another hot California night.

Gil lit up a joint, one for him, one for me. He rolled two more.

I could see he was in for intense smoking.

I took some puffs of mine, more to keep him company than to get high.

When he'd smoked half of his first joint, he spoke:

"I made love to you last night after you'd passed out." He looked guilty. I realized I'd never even seen Gil look guilty, but apparently he'd finally done something that even he didn't approve of. "I just wanted to see if I could do it before you came to," he said.

Somehow passing out *while* making love was one thing—at least it implied my consent. But doing it *after* I'd passed out, without my agreeing to it—that was something else again.

I sat at the bottom of my geek pit, sickened. I was beyond rage.

"You made love to me and I wasn't even there?" I felt like my whole life was happening to me and I wasn't even there.

Gil nodded.

"There's a name for people who make love to dead bodies!" With that I stood up, stripped off my jeans and T-shirt and walked stark naked straight into the Pacific Ocean.

It was full of brilliant green fluorescent phosphorus (for some reason known as "red tide") and wherever I put my foot the water around it lit up like lime green neon.

I walked out into deeper water. There was a strong undertow—I'd seen warning signs along the beach all week telling swimmers to stay close to shore.

I walked out even further.

Gil remained sitting cross-legged on his beach towel, puffing away at his marijuana cigarette.

In water up to my waist, I ducked down and disappeared under the surface, just like I used to do as a kid.

The undertow sucked at my body and I swam down to meet it. A cold tug from a current of a different temperature dragged me further into it. The fluorescent green neon was gone now and there was only black. I let myself be carried up where a huge wave got me, wrenched me away from the undertow, and dumped me back onto the beach. I stood up and dove right back in through the next wave, pulling myself down into the undertow where again it went from green neon to the blackest black. The time Barney and I were up over the Santa Monica Mountains in the Cessna in thick fog crossed my mind. I'd been disoriented: Which was up and which was down?

"If our radio goes out now, we're up shit creek without a paddle," Barney had said, hardly disguising how thrilled he was to be caught in such an adventure.

Then I'd been scared.

Now I didn't even care.

My ears had so much sand in them that I couldn't hear. Over and over I let my naked body get dragged out to sea by the undertow and then I'd find myself being tossed back on shore where I'd see Gil, still sitting in the lotus position on his towel, oblivious.

What brought me back was a thin little thought that pushed up into my consciousness from somewhere like a blade of grass through a concrete sidewalk: Emily and Abby need me.

At this very moment those two little girls, my children, were sleeping upstairs in their beds unaware that down here on the dark beach their mother was playing drowning games.

This was the only motivation I had to live, the silver thread between death and me—not death from disappointment but from real drowning.

But it was enough.

I pulled myself out of the water, walked up onto the cold sand and fell onto my towel next to Gil.

"You looked absolutely beautiful out there, all naked with your hair wet and tangled. Beautiful!"

"Thanks."

"Like a sea nymph. You gave me such a hard-on you have no idea."

"You should have been a lifeguard," I said sarcastically.

It went right over his head.

I lay there looking at the moon behind Gil's head like a halo. He was still puffing away on his weed, holding his breath now to keep the precious smoke in his lungs.

I had just decided to go on living, but I was still at the bottom of my geek pit waiting for my nightly reward.

What the hell, I asked myself, do I do now?

I got my immediate answer from that mindreader, Gil:

"What do you say we go inside and fuck."

# – 20 –

## MESSAGE SENT ISN'T ALWAYS
## MESSAGE RECEIVED

*Until the mind is ready to see something,*
*it will go unnoticed.*
*—Ovid, 17 A.D.*

I don't think messengers or "Eskimos" who lead us back to civilization are put in our path for the express purpose of teaching us something. I think they're probably there all the time, only we just don't see them until we're ready.

For me, Harlan Yates had been a messenger. When he spoke, I listened. Maybe because he was cute. Some of us need cute messengers.

Nearly two years earlier the woman at the cocktail party who volunteered that she was an alcoholic—and now sober—could have been an Eskimo, but I wasn't ready for her. I went out of my way to avoid her. Yet, without intending to, I'd filed away her message for future reference.

Harlan showed me that I had feelings, not just an intellect. He also showed me that my life wasn't working. Gil showed me that I had a sexual nature and that one of the reasons my body as well as my life wasn't working right was because of something called "drinking." He actually *named* the problem. But once it was named, neither of us knew what to do about it.

The messenger who told me what to do about it was Billy O'Neal.

Billy O'Neal was an artist who did wild and angry seascapes. I'd met him a few times at Barney's airport. He was one of Barney's flying students.

I bumped into him one chilly, overcast Saturday afternoon at a parking lot art show in the Marina. I'd gone there so I wouldn't stay home and brood about Gil and Gudren who'd gone off camping together taking *my* sleeping bag with them—another geeky thing I had to swallow.

Billy O'Neal didn't look in the least bit artistic. If anything, he looked like Mafia with his large, solid build and beady black eyes. He had an aura of violence about him, although as far as I knew he'd never hurt anybody.

He was standing in front of his seascapes, hands thrust into the pockets of his black leather jacket.

I said hello and reminded him who I was.

"I remember you," he said. "You were with Barney."

"We broke up."

"Relationships suck."

Billy suddenly leapt for one of his paintings which had just been caught by a gust of wind. The wind had been picking up steadily for the last hour and now threatened to blow the whole art show over.

"Goddamn!" he said, getting it just in time.

He was clearly in a foul mood.

"You look like you could use a drink!" I said, being cute.

"Interesting thought—but I'm a recovering alcoholic, so I don't think a very *good* one."

I didn't expect that. He'd just told me more about himself than I wanted to know. I must have physically recoiled.

"Don't worry, you can't catch it!"

Without hesitating I said: "I think I already *have*." It just popped out.

"Meaning?"

"Meaning I think I have a drinking problem."

I hadn't anticipated saying that either. This was turning into a very strange conversation.

Billy didn't flinch. "If you think you do, you probably do," he said casually.

The instant he said that I felt relieved. At least he was taking me seriously. He didn't tell me I was "silly" worrying about a drinking problem.

Now of course in my mind the issue here was only that—a "drinking problem"—and not what he said he had—alcoholism. Alcoholism was a whole different thing in my book.

"Did you ever get your pilot's license?" he asked. Billy didn't seem any more eager to pursue the subject than I was.

I shook my head.

"How come?"

"The night flying lessons were coming up and since I drink at night I didn't think that would be safe. So I quit the lessons."

I'd just told the truth. What a wild feeling!

Billy laughed. "What are you going to do about the drinking?"

"I don't know yet. What did you do?"

"A recovery group."

I thought about that a minute. "Will you take me?"

Billy shook his head. "Sorry, rescuing maidens isn't my trip."

"How do I find one?"

"Try the phone book."

"Oh, okay." I'd never have thought of that if he hadn't said it.

I didn't see Billy again for five years.

In the Yellow Pages I ran across a listing for the National Council on Alcoholism. That sounded sort of scholarly and appealed to me. I figured that even though they specialized in alcoholism (which wasn't my problem), they still might be able to give me some pointers about my drinking—like how to cut down.

I wrote down the address and phone number of a local office and stuck it in my wallet. I carried it around with me for another six weeks.

And I kept right on drinking.

But I felt better just knowing the information was there.

I didn't know what I was waiting for until it happened: my day in court. I was waiting until I had my divorce and legal custody of Emily and Abby. I didn't want any messy labels involving alcohol until all that was behind me.

My court date came—nine o'clock on a Monday morning.

I was there—hungover, but punctual.

Little did I know that this was my last hangover. Had I known, I might have paid some attention to it, arranged a little fanfare. But on that morning it was just another hangover from just another night of drinking too much gin and I treated it the same old way: Valium and aspirin.

The divorce proceeding went off like clockwork and by 9:10 I was walking back down the courthouse steps, my children (for whom I'd recently pulled myself out of the Pacific Ocean) officially in my custody. They were *my* responsibility now.

When I reached the bottom of the courthouse steps, a thought went through my head: *Today's the day.*

Two hours later I was sitting in front of a woman named Ruth at the National Council on Alcoholism.

"It's the strangest thing, even though I'm not an alcoholic, I still can't seem to control my drinking." I didn't want to misrepresent myself, so I felt it was only fair to tell her this up front. "I drink sometimes even when I don't want to drink. It's like I drink against my will."

She listened patiently as I rattled on. I was afraid that at any moment she was going to throw me out for wasting her time with a mere drinking problem when they had real problems, alcoholism problems, to attend to. But I had the sense that without help, I was done for. "I'm here because I know I can't do it alone."

I told myself if she did kick me out I could always picket!

"I don't drink during the day the way alcoholics do, but at night I'm like Pavlov's dog. Suddenly around five o'clock the urge to drink hits me and I drink even when I've *promised* myself I won't do it. I do it anyway and then I can't stop until I fall asleep, which is pretty early."

I was sure that all of this I was telling her was unique, something she'd never run into before—a non-alcoholic who is compelled to drink.

"We call that alcoholism."

I was dumbfounded.

"No! It *is*? That's what alcoholism is? You mean a drinking problem and alcoholism are the same thing?"

"Yes, usually," she said.

It was mind-boggling.

"You're *sure*?"

She picked up a yellow card the size of a business envelope and handed it to me. "This is called the Twenty Question Test for Alcoholism," she said. She folded the bottom part underneath so I couldn't see it. "Maybe it'll help you decided. Check yes or no by each one. Be as honest as you can."

"Okay."

When I took the pencil my hand shook. Ruth noticed it.

"That's withdrawal," she said matter-of-factly. "When was your last drink?"

"Last night."

"Yeah, that's it."

And all this time I'd thought I shook because I was such a deep and sensitive person.

"Was your last drink before midnight?"

"Yes."

"Then this is your first day of sobriety."

The very idea struck me as absurd. Nobody can just get sober—poof! like that—without first finding out *why* they drink so they can stop needing it. Ruth and I hadn't talked about my childhood or my feelings or any of that. To me "sober" was something that might be years down the road, not *now*.

But I didn't want to argue with her, so I said nothing.

I picked up the Twenty Question Test and began to read the first one:

1. *Do you lose time from work due to drinking?* Hmmm? Stuck already! How do I answer this? You answer by telling the truth, Sylvia! Let's see, my hours at the photo studio are my own, and I get there late a lot (hungover)—so I guess that's "losing time." Plus a lot of mornings I'm so shaky I have to take Valium before I can pick up a camera. I guess that's "losing time." And I sit around and smoke cigarettes and procrastinate instead of work—and I only feel ambitious in spurts. And then there's all those wasted evenings... I checked YES.

2. *Is drinking making your home life unhappy?* What home life! Gil is always out screwing around! (But *why* is he out screwing around Sylvia? Because you drink, that's why! Tit for tat.) And drinking had a lot to do with the marriage to Sandy going bad—and has a lot to do with the quality of mothering going on...Answer: YES.

3. *Do you drink because you are shy with other people?* I put NO. I had no idea why I drank, but I didn't think it was shyness. Besides, whenever I went to a party I always had my "get-dressed martini" beforehand so even if I was shy, I didn't give myself a chance to feel it!

4. *Is drinking affecting your reputation?* At first I put NO—then erased it when I figured out "reputation" means what the people who know you think of you. Drinking most certainly had affected my reputation—with Sandy, with my mother, with my in-laws (cringe), with Mrs. Owens, with Emily's psychiatrist (cringe again), with Barney, with my NOW associates (cringe), with headwaiters, with my former literary agent (although she didn't know gin was the culprit), with Veda, and now with Gil. Answer: YES.

5. *Have you ever felt remorse after drinking?* Easy—all the time. Guilty, guilty, guilty! I felt guilty all the time—because I was. I put a YES.

131

6. *Have you ever gotten into financial difficulties as the result of drinking?* I put NO immediately. Lie! I wasn't making a cent. I'd stopped writing. I'd lost my book contract. I'd given up psychology forever—and now I was losing, not making, money at the photo studio. Sandy's alimony and child-support were my "income" and without that I'd most definitely have been in financial difficulties. I had a lot to learn about self-deceit.

7. *Do you turn to lower companions and an inferior environment when drinking?* Answer NO. (Semi-lie!) Mostly I drank alone at home, so my "lower companion" was myself—and occasionally Veda (although I didn't think she'd appreciate being called a lower companion!) And my inferior environment was my own home where I'd wake up to the smell of stale booze from the glass on the bedside table and stale cigarettes. This probably should have been a YES.

8. *Does your drinking make you careless of your family's welfare?* (Cringe!) I'd say giving little girls shampoos while in a blackout—or driving children around after I'd been drinking—or falling down drunk in the kid's room and lying there all night crying, (which scared them to death) was being careless of their welfare. I put YES.

9. *Has your ambition decreased since drinking?* Never thought of it before, but YES. I reviewed some of the things I'd stopped doing since I started drinking—the writing, the projects, the decorating, the sewing, the trips, the reading, the physical exercise—even the desire for these things—all gone. Answer: YES.

10. *Do you crave a drink at a definite time daily?* YES, when it's five o'clock somewhere!

11. *Do you want a drink the next morning?* I put NO. I didn't know about the "hair of the dog" cure. My hair-of-the-dog was Valium.

12. *Does drinking cause you to have difficulty in sleeping?* I almost put NO because gin was what *put* me to sleep—that or Valium. But I always woke up too early, sometimes in the middle of the night, and then I couldn't go back to sleep. I considered *that* a sleeping problem, so I put YES.

13. *Has your efficiency decreased since drinking?* I'd never thought of that, either—but now that I did, definitely YES. This test was uncovering a lot of stuff I'd kept secret from myself.

14. *Is drinking jeopardizing your job or business?* I put NO. (Lying again!) I'd already drunk myself out of a writing career and out of a career as a revolutionary! If I'd been on salary at the photo studio

instead of paying to work there, Hank would probably have canned me. I was not as promising a student as he'd hoped for.

15. *Do you drink to escape from worries or troubles?* Again, these "why" questions threw me. I had no idea why I drank. I just drank, that's all. I did it like it was Mount Everest—because it was there. And if it wasn't there, I'd go buy some. So I put NO.

16. *Do you drink alone?* Answer: YES.

17. *Have you ever had a complete loss of memory (blacked-out) as the result of drinking?* Oh, I thought, is *that* what "falling asleep early" is really called? A blackout? Interesting! YES.

18. *Has your physician ever treated you for drinking?* I put NO. I forgot about all those in-conclusive tests I'd had for stomach pains—the pains that later went away after I'd stopped drinking.

19. *Do you drink to build up your self-confidence?* There's another of those silly "why" questions. I don't know—so NO.

20. *Have you ever been to a hospital or institution on account of drinking?* Answer: NO. (Real answer: Not yet.) A chemical dependency unit is a hospital. And jail for a drunk driving arrest is an "institution." A loony bin is also an "institution." Court is an "institution." They were all out there waiting for me.

When I finished, I looked up at Ruth.

"Count your Yes answers."

I did. "Only fourteen," I said, handing her my card.

She laughed.

She unfolded the bottom part and read it to me: "If you have answered YES to any one of the questions, there is a warning that you may be an alcoholic. If you have answered YES to any two, the chances are that you are an alcoholic. If you have answered YES to three or more, you are definitely an alcoholic."

My reaction to this was not: "Oh, no!" or "Not true!" My reaction was: "I passed!"

I felt relief. "So *that's* what I am! So that's what's wrong with me—*alcoholism.*"

When I'd merely had a "neurotic drinking problem" there was no hope because there was only one place you go for that—to a psychiatrist, and I'd already gone that route. It hadn't worked.

But for alcoholism (which Ruth had explained was a real disease) there were lots of places to go. I'd seen some of them listed in the Yellow Pages.

For alcoholism there was hope. (Until that moment I didn't realize I'd lost it.)

And I wouldn't have to picket or fight anymore.

"Can I keep this card?"

"Of course."

I stuck it in my purse where it would remain for months—just in case someone dared question my claim to being a real alcoholic. I could whip out the card and say, "Here, look! I got fourteen YESes and all you need is *three*!"

Ruth gave me a number of referrals for help, from inpatient hospitalization to private shrinks to self-help groups. I chose a nationwide self-help group and she picked out a local meeting for me to go to that night.

She had me call Gil right from her desk to ask him to babysit the kids so I could go to the meeting. He agreed. He was pleased I'd finally turned myself in.

Next Ruth instructed me to take the girls out to dinner so I didn't have to be in the house before the meeting. "I don't want Pavlov's dog to bite you before you get there," she said. "Five o'clock will be your worst time of day for a while but that will pass."

I couldn't believe we were both sitting there having this conversation and making these plans. I listened intently and took in every word she said like a sponge. If she'd told me to wear purple spandex pants to my first meeting I'd have done it.

"Please call me tomorrow morning and let me know how it went."

I said I would, not knowing my chances of surviving all this were probably about one in thirty-five.

I bounced down the stairs and out onto the street. I wanted to shout out: Can you believe it?! I'm an alcoholic! That's what was wrong with me all this time!

It's only alcoholism!

# – 21 –

# THE FLASH EXPERIENCE

*When your legs give out, that's it.*
*—William Wyler*

I followed Ruth's directions like a trained seal. At 5:30 I picked up
Emily and Abby from their after-school daycare. At 5:45 the three of
us were sitting at a table at Burger King to keep me out of trouble
until it was time for my recovery group meeting.

I looked at all the people who were out loose at cocktail hour and
imagined that they were also looking at me and saying to themselves,
"Wow, there's a woman who's not home drinking."

But I *wanted* to be home drinking.

Being on my way to a meeting was irrelevant. The push to drink
was still there, as much a part of me as an organ in my body. I could
look inside myself and almost feel it. There was my heart, my lungs,
my kidneys, my liver—and my alcoholism.

As long as it was there, I knew I'd drink again.

By 6:45 we'd finished eating. At 7:00 we were home. Gil's van
was in the driveway. I was afraid to go in. I sent the girls scampering
up the outside staircase and waited until Gil appeared on the balcony
in his native outfit, cut-off jeans and holding a joint.

"I am *so* nervous!" I shouted at him from below, competing with
the sound of the waves on the beach. "What if it's awful? What if it
doesn't work? How can a meeting help? What if it's all Skid Row
bums sitting around a fire?"

"In April?"

"What if somebody sees me there?"

135

"'He who worries in advance gets to experience it twice,'" Gil answered.

In the car on the way to Westwood, I took a Valium out of my purse and swallowed it—waterlessly.

Inside I was on the cutting edge of desperation: This *had* to work. It was my only hope. If it didn't work I'd be (as Barney would have said) up shit creek without a paddle.

I might even die.

When I walked into a little clubhouse jammed with about two hundred chattering people, it felt more like a cocktail party than a meeting for drunks. It also struck me as wildly funny to see all those dressed-up men and women drinking coffee instead of cocktails—like a styrofoam cup commercial.

A door-greeter shook my hand. "You must be new."

I was thinking, How does he know that? when he said, "Your *hand* is clammy."

"Oh. Sorry."

"It'll pass. Welcome."

I found a seat in the back.

The meeting was scheduled to begin at 8:30—and it did. Punctuality, I was to learn, is part of the spiritual path.

When the woman at the podium introduced herself as an alcoholic, I slid down in my seat out of embarrassment for her—saying such a thing in public! I thought it meant she was still drinking; I expected her to stagger. But she meant *recovering* alcoholic.

The main speaker was a TV actor. Of course I didn't recognize him since I hadn't been sober late enough in the evening to watch TV in years.

I enjoyed him. He was funny. He made me laugh. It was like being at the theater.

But in spite of all this, I could still feel my alcoholism gnawing away inside of me like an inflamed organ, lying in wait.

As I looked around the room at all the sober people, a thought wafted across my mind and got my attention: "They're sober; I'm not. I think I'll listen and do what they say."

With that trigger sentence—a throwaway line really—I felt something shift inside and in a flash (which is why later on I called it my "flash experience") my whole world view changed. And I'd done nothing on purpose to make that happen.

136

In a "flash" my conscious world seemed to expand outward and I felt, clichéd though it sounds, that a burden was lifted. I didn't even believe in quick cures and yet I know I'd had one! (Since then I've seen thousands of similar instant recoveries.)

One moment I'd been a little ship lost at sea on a dark night. Then a flash of lightning lit up the sky and showed me where shore was and for the very first time in my life I knew I had a destination.

All I had to do now was make the trip.

And most amazing of all was the fact that when I looked inside me for that familiar old alcoholism "organ" I'd felt only moments before, it was gone.

Poof! Just like that.

And I knew I was going to be able to stop drinking immediately—something I'd expected would take me years. In place of that urge was commitment—I was suddenly "struck"—committed.

It was wild.

I raced home to tell Gil the news:

"I'm cured!"

He was sitting cross-legged on the beanbag, eating a Twinkie and listening to the Rolling Stones.

"Isn't that a little quick?"

"No, really, it's true!"

"Sylvia, there's no such thing as an overnight cure."

"But it happened."

"That's snake oil stuff."

"I know you think that, but I can feel it, right in *here*." I pointed to my stomach.

Gil shook his head. "Other than that, Mrs. Lincoln, how did you enjoy the play?"

I ignored that. I rushed on to tell him more: "Gil, it blew my mind. I didn't know something like that could even happen. One second I was an alcoholic and the next second I wasn't. My therapist used to tell me I could choose not to drink, but I couldn't. Not ever. But tonight I could. I said to myself, I can drink—or I can *not* drink. And I just decided I wouldn't. And I don't care how hard it is going to be, I know I can do it. Even if it's painful, I can stand it. I can stand *any*thing!"

Gil took a bite of his Twinkie. He was looking more uncomfortable by the minute. Finally he interrupted me.

"You know," he said, "it would be nice if you could do this thing without using a recovery group as a crutch."

For a moment I felt as though I'd been punched in the stomach and then thrown back into that geek pit where I belonged.

Only this time I landed on my feet.

"Go to hell!" I said.

I waited impatiently to go back to the recovery group meeting the following week. I didn't drink. I had no idea there were other meetings I could have gone to—*should* have gone to.

The only trouble I had was sleeping. I'd usually counted on gin to knock me out. Without that I was wakeful, so I took Valium. Then to wake up in the morning I took Dexedrine. To get high I smoked grass. Plus Gil and I made serious plans to take another LSD trip.

And I thought I was sober.

Compared to where I'd come from, I was. No more hangovers. No more blackouts. No more lost weeknights. I enjoyed the sunshine in my bedroom in the mornings now and I didn't even mind the birds, the ones my stepfather used to call those "goddamned chirpie-chirpies at the crack of doom."

I was still scared Pavlov's dog would strike me drunk so during that first week I steered clear of the house between five and seven o'clock. On the second night of my sobriety, we dined at Denny's. On the third night, Jack in the Box. On the fourth night, McDonald's. On the fifth, Taco Bell. And on the sixth night we went to Chasen's where I ate the spinach salad instead of falling asleep in it.

When Monday night rolled around again, I assumed Gil would babysit so I could go to my meeting.

Instead Gil balked.

"Why should I babysit *your* kids so you can go gallivanting around?"

That was geek pit treatment again.

I got a babysitter and went.

What was bothering Gil was my sobriety. By getting sober I'd gone and changed the game. We had a tit-for-tat deal that gave him permission to fool around when I drank—and now I'd stopped drinking. It threw him.

One night he came over for dinner. When he'd finished eating, he stood up. "Well, I'm off."

"Where the hell are you going?"

"Out."

"To do what?"

"See Gudren."

"Oh, really?"

"We have an arrangement, remember?"

"Not for you to come over here and eat first, we don't! How *dare* you do that! I'm not your goddamned mother!"

I was furious. How delicious it was to feel righteous indignation after all those years of drinking. When you're drinking, even when you're *right* you're wrong!

"Don't you ever pull something like that on me again!"

I meant it. Gil knew I meant it.

Grinning sheepishly, he stood up and headed for the front door. But first he stopped to grab an apple from the fruit bowl on the coffee table, just like a kid brazenly swiping something knowing perfectly well an adult is watching.

He sailed out the front door, down the stairs and off across the beach, chewing on the apple.

After two and a half weeks I told Sandy I'd stopped drinking. He wasn't overly impressed:

"Well, let's see now. First there was psychology. Then writing. Then women's lib. Then marriage and motherhood in there somewhere. Then Gestalt therapy. Then photography. And now sobriety. I wonder what the next fad will be?"

I decided to shut up about my snake oil cure until more time had gone by.

At the end of my first month, I went to one of my recovery group meetings and during the coffee break I cornered Pauline, a woman who'd become a sort of mentor, and gushed about how much I loved being sober. "But to tell you the truth, Pauline, if it weren't for the Valium I'd have a dreadful time sleeping."

"You take Valium?"

"Yes. But just to sleep."

"Then you're not sober."

I must have looked as deflated as a night sky suddenly captured by a black hole. I could feel my whole body cave in.

"What do you mean?"

"I'm sorry, Sylvia dear. Around here sobriety means no mind-altering chemicals. But you're certainly welcome to keep coming to meetings as a visitor. Nobody's going to kick you out."

"Pauline, I want to be *sober*." I was holding back tears.

"Then no more Valium."

"What about grass?"

"Grass too? No grass. Grass is mind-altering."

"Dexedrine?"

She shook her head.

"Does LSD count?"

She smiled. Apparently I was amusing her.

"I'd say LSD is mind-altering, wouldn't you?"

"Wow," I said.

This was beginning to look like a whole different ball game.

# – 22 –

# THE LAST ONE PERCENT

*Happiness is not a reward—it is a consequence.*
*Suffering is not a punishment—it is a result.*
—*R. G. Ingersoll*
The Christian Religion

That night I went cold turkey off of Valium.

Like a lot of people, I had no idea Valium would be so rough to detox from on my own—and I was only on a little. Probably I should have had medical help or been hospitalized—for both alcohol and Valium withdrawal, but I didn't even think of it.

I went and did it myself. And not once did I think: "To hell with it." The commitment feeling I'd gotten as the result of the "flash experience" process struck again. I knew I was committed to total sobriety, despite pain, despite nerves, despite anxiety. "We don't drink and we don't use no matter what," they told me and I repeated that to myself over and over—like a mantra. Again, it was "instant cure" and it astounded me—but later I realized how common this experience is—under different names such as conversion experience, moment of clarity, surrender, turning point, grace, born-again, spontaneous remission, insight, etc. In a "readied" individual, anything can trigger such a healing experience and even though I didn't know it, I was ready.

For two weeks I hardly slept. All everyday sensations seemed intensified. Colors were more colorful, anger was angrier, noises noisier, smells smellier, sadness sadder. When Harlan told me about the wonderful world of feelings he didn't tell me the half of it! There were times when life was so unrelentingly stimulating that all I wanted to do was crawl into the box I'd arrived in and have them ship me back.

141

I tried every folk remedy for sleep the recovery group people and health food stores would tell me about—hot baths, warm milk, onion sandwiches, reading boring books, camomile tea.

"You can't die from lack of sleep," Pauline said.

"That would look like *up* from here," I said.

In the middle of all this I called Gil to cancel our scheduled LSD trip.

"Those people are sure messing with your head. LSD can't hurt you, Sylvia, it's not like alcohol. All it can do is make you more creative. Are they against that too? Did you tell them you're a writer?"

"I'm sorry, Gil. I just can't."

"I think you're making a mistake."


Finally the night came when I fell asleep at a reasonable hour, about 2 a.m., and awoke at eight.

I felt wonderful.

The cobwebs had cleared. The gauze filter between me and life was gone. I had a new clarity. It was like climbing a ladder and looking down on my life from a different perspective. I found myself looking around and saying, "I need this in my life. I *don't* need that in my life."

One of the things I decided I didn't need was Gil.

Gil, because of his attitude and drug use, was now a threat to my sobriety and had to go. Maybe it seemed ruthless, but in the recovery group everything was seen in terms of life and death—and I loved it, this talk about raw survival.

I was determined to be a survivor. It was a word that always excited me. Even as a kid I loved survival stories. I collected books on survival: survival in the desert; survival in the jungle; survival at sea; survival in the arctic. I read them as if they were novels. What would *I* do if I were shipwrecked on a deserted island? I ate it all up.

Now even standing up for myself and telling people my feelings instead of stuffing them was linked up with survival. If I didn't confront people and if I swallowed my hurt or pain, I'd brood and if I brooded too much I might drink and if I drank I might die.

Now I gave myself permission to do what up until then had been so hard for me: treat myself and my life with a little respect.

I told Gil it was over.

He wasn't surprised. He'd seen it coming. This gave him an excuse to do what he'd been wanting to do for years—skip town.

He quit his airline job, sent Jamie to live with his mother in Michigan (and her latest truck driver) and, armed with a backpack, camera and a free plane ticket, set out to hitchhike around the world.

I took him to the airport and put him on a plane to Tokyo. When he disappeared through the gate, I felt relief.

Now I was alone.

Now that I was clean and sober, off of *all* mind-altering chemicals, I became obsessed with going to recovery group meetings—between six and nine of them a week.

I alternated three regular babysitters.

Big Roberta was my Tuesday-Thursday-Sunday sitter. She was only fourteen but was six feet tall so I felt safe having her watch the kids. She looked so fierce.

One night I was all set to leave for my meeting when Big Roberta appeared at my screen door, breathless and in tears.

"I just came over to tell you I had a fight with my Dad and I'm grounded. He's stupid drunk. God, I hate that!"

"You can't sit?" My heart started pounding as the meaning of all this started to become clear. Panic. How was I going to get to my meeting?

Suddenly Big Roberta's father was standing beside her at the door. He was a head shorter and obviously angry. I couldn't tell he was drunk from looking at him. But I could smell it. He was pulling at her arm and she was resisting.

"You're grounded, lady. Get the hell home!"

"Daddy, please let me sit!"

"Harry, please let her sit!"

"Not a chance. Roberta, go home."

"But I have to go out. It's *very* important to me!"

He yanked Roberta down the stairs.

I ran after them—down the stairs and out to the street.

"Harry, you can't do that! It's not fair!"

It was useless.

Off they went down the block, Harry pulling a resistant Big Roberta behind him like an unbroken horse.

Suddenly I escalated into a rage. How dare he do this to me! How dare he interfere with my plans!

I stormed back upstairs, slammed the front door, yelled at the cat, screamed at the kids (who'd been innocently blissed out in their bubble bath), banged pots, clanged dishes, kicked over a kitchen chair. My heart was thumping, my blood was racing.

I *had* to get to that meeting. I *had* to, *had* to, *had* to!

Finally I had the presence of mind to call Pauline: "How dare that son-of-a-bitch be so inconsiderate! How the hell am I supposed to get to my meeting? I *have* to get to my meeting!"

"My, we sure do want what we want when we want it, don't we?" she said teasingly.

"But I'm stuck here!"

"It looks like you are. It looks like maybe tonight you're meant to stay home and be with your children."

Meant to? What did she mean, "meant to"? I didn't like that meant-to kind of talk. It sounded churchy. Who did I have on the other end of this phone, anyway, a nun? In the old days I would have blitzed her right out of my life for less than that.

"You don't understand, Pauline," I said, trying to sound like I wasn't having the thoughts I was having. "I can't stay home. I'm nervous!"

"Are you going to drink?"

"Of course not!" The thought hadn't even occurred to me. That fact alone was a miracle, but I missed it.

"Then what are you afraid of?"

I thought about that for a moment: "My feelings!"

"Feelings won't kill you. Gin will. You can be alone with your feelings and not die."

"I was alone with them for years!"

"No. You had gin."

Immediately I felt myself calm down. If Pauline said I'd be okay then I knew I'd be okay—and she wasn't even a therapist. Pauline was just a defrocked nurse who'd lost her license once upon a long time ago due to booze and never got it back.

"Look at it this way," Pauline went on to say. "Maybe God has something for you to learn tonight and staying home is the only way you can learn it."

"Oh, Pauline!" This time I couldn't keep my mouth shut. "You know how I hate that God-talk!"

"Yes, I do know," she said. "I'm just giving you an opportunity to work on one of your character defects."

"*What* character defect?" That was such an archaic term. "What are you referring to?"

"Judgmentalness."

Swallow.

"I'll be home tonight myself, so call me if it gets hairy. Otherwise I'll talk to you tomorrow. And Sylvia?"

"What?"

"Please remember that I love you and you're going to be fine."

I felt tears fill my eyes. I was glad she couldn't see. I would have been embarrassed to show her I was touched.

"Thanks, Pauline."


For the first hour I was antsy. Emily and Abby were pleased to have me home unexpectedly and were clingy and demanding. We made cookies (I had a sweet tooth now and had gained nearly ten pounds). We licked the bowls and I poured myself a diet Pepsi over ice. I had to have liquids within arm's reach all the time—at work, at home, in the car. And I still gulped them.

Later on Abby settled down in the middle of the living room floor with her crayons and coloring books. But Emily, who'd picked up my antsy vibes, started fussing over the back seam in her jeans which was suddenly too bumpy. Her skin was still so super-sensitive I'd taken to calling her "Princess and the Pea."

"Get these *off* of me!" she screeched.

"You being Princess?"

"Stop!" She knew I was teasing her.

"You're weird, Em," Abby put in her two cents. She knew just how to inflame Emily, who now began to cry and kick at Abby's crayons. Abby grabbed her ankle.

I decided to intervene.

"Emily, come here and let Mommy help you get out of those phoffy pants."

Emily loved silly words and tonight they worked like a charm. She stood patiently in front of me and let me free her from her jeans. When she was in her flowered cotton underpants and T-shirt she was happy.

"How 'bout sitting in Mommy's lap and watching the sailboats with me?"

That was asking a lot from Emily. She wasn't a lap child. That was one of the things "in the direction of autism" about her. Usually she'd stiffen and pull away.

But tonight she crawled right up into my lap. Before she let herself sit back, she leaned over and sniffed at my glass of diet Pepsi.

She was checking it out for gin!

Dumb like a fox!

Then she leaned her slim little body back into me. I felt her relax. Then, gingerly, not wanting to scare her off, I put my arms around her and held her. She didn't pull away. She found a piece of her long, tangly hair and sucked on it. Abby, seeing there would be no more opportunities for excitement, went back to her coloring.

I gazed out over Emily's head through the large picture window that overlooked the beach and the ocean. The sun was setting and the atmospheric dust made it look like a huge orange beach ball sitting on the horizon. Sailboats with multicolored sails criss-crossed in front of it. It took willpower for me to just sit there and enjoy it instead of jumping up to photograph it.

It was a glorious sight and as I continued to enjoy it, the whole scene seemed to get brighter, almost luminescent, and the objects glowed with a life of their own.

I noticed my breathing and how good it felt. Not since that LSD trip with Gil had I been aware of enjoying just breathing in and breathing out. It was sensuous. It was ecstasy.

Just sitting there holding Emily on my lap and stroking her hair and seeing Abby's little foot sticking out from under her nightgown made my chest feel warm, as though filled with liquid gold.

What else could anyone possibly want?

I thought of the night I'd played the drowning game down there on the beach, toying with my life as if it were valueless. And I remembered that thin thread of a thought that had pulled me back up on shore: My children need me.

All of a sudden I realized that this strange new sensation I was having was a feeling—the one feeling I had been sure I was incapable of experiencing.

It was the feeling called love.

# – 23 –

# LOVE AND WORK

*All who take this remedy recover in a short time except
those whom it does not help, who all die and have no relief
from any other medicine. Therefore, it is obvious that it
fails only in incurable cases.*
— *Galen, physician, second century A.D.*

*That which doesn't kill me makes me stronger.*
— *Nietzsche*

Freud said when love and work are going well, you've got your act together. My life was a shambles in both areas.

I remember saying to myself at around three months of sobriety: My name is Sylvia and I'm an alcoholic—and that's all I know. Everything else is up for grabs. I don't know if I'm a Democrat or a Republican, if I like movies or hate TV, what my favorite color is or if I'm outgoing or shy. I don't even know what I want to be when I grow up.

I envied those people who knew what they wanted to be from the age of nine-and-three-quarters. It wasn't like that for me. I found out what I wanted to be by eliminating all the things I *didn't* want to be and seeing what was left.

That meant trying a lot of things.

Being in the photography business wasn't proving profitable. I kept giving things away. I gave away my time. I gave away my ideas. I gave away my products: "Here are six free enlargements for your friends!"

Once a woman walked into the studio with her little daughter. She wanted a single 5 x 7-inch black and white picture of the child for the grandmother's birthday. "How much?" she asked.

"Fifteen dollars," I said.

She frowned. "But I just want you to *snap* a picture."

Immediately I felt guilty for charging fifteen dollars for just snapping a picture, a mere 1/125th of a second's work. At $15.00 for 1/125th of a second, that would be $1875 for a full second, $112,500 for a minute and $6,750,000 for an hour—$6,750,000 an hour was too much.

"Okay, five dollars."

I "snapped" a roll of thirty-six pictures (half an hour's work), spent an hour processing the film and making a proof sheet. Then I phoned the woman to come in and select the shot she wanted. Then I spent another half hour enlarging the print, drying it and mounting it.

In the middle of it I caught on that I'd just screwed myself.

Standing at the tubs in the darkroom, I reached for the phone and dialed Pauline's number by touch.

"How could I have *done* this to myself!" I wailed. "I'm so angry. Why couldn't I just tell her it's fifteen dollars or *else*?"

"One, you're a people-pleaser. Two, you lack self-worth."

"Three, I'm an asshole!"

"People don't get well in style."

"What do I do, Pauline?"

"You give her the picture for five dollars like you said you would, and next time you start thinking like the diamond cutter in the story."

"What story?"

"The one I'm about to tell you, so listen. Once upon a time there was a diamond cutter who cut a diamond and then presented his customer with a bill for $3010. The customer looked at the bill and said: 'Three thousand and *ten* dollars? What's the ten dollars for?' 'The ten dollars is for cutting the diamond,' the diamond cutter said. 'The three thousand dollars is for knowing where to cut.'"

"I love it! So I should have charged her five dollars for snapping the picture and three thousand for knowing when to snap!"

"Something like that, Sylvia. But it's going to be a while before you can do that. In the meantime I suggest you find a job where they force a paycheck on you at the end of the week whether you feel you're a worthy person or not."

"You mean work in an *office*?"

Pauline could hear the contempt in my voice.

"After I lost my license I scrubbed toilets."

"God, Pauline, I'm so sorry."

"Don't be sorry. It was a spiritual experience."

I laughed. I had no idea that she was serious.

One evening I went to Sandy's new apartment in West Hollywood to pick up Emily and Abby. Sandy had thrown himself into being a bachelor. He frequented nightclubs and topless joints along Sunset Strip. He was also less depressed. I suspected a relationship.

"You're looking wonderful," he said.

"I'm still sober."

"That's terrific. I'm proud of you."

When he said that I was happy. At least now he wasn't assuming that sobriety was just a passing fancy.

On impulse, I decided to make my amends to him. The recovery group encouraged us to tell all the people we'd hurt with our drinking that we were sorry.

"I'm sorry for the things I did that hurt you and hurt our marriage," I said. "You didn't deserve it. You were a wonderful husband to me. I'm glad I was married to you. I'm glad that Emily and Abby have you for a father."

Sandy's eyes filled with tears, only this time they were the happy kind. He reached out and squeezed my hand.

"Thank you for saying that, Sylvia. That meant a lot to me—maybe more than you could possibly know."

That was the start of the healing between us.


Then I began to job hunt. Naturally, I went to the want-ads in the *Los Angeles Times*. I discovered they were no longer segregated into Help Wanted: Male and Help Wanted: Female. When did that happen?

These Rip Van Winkle experiences threw me. Where had I been? (Answer: Drinking.)

I felt proud that I'd had something to do with the integrated want-ads. Someday if Emily or Abby wanted to know what Mommy did in the revolution, I could point to that.


The job I got was in a hospital doing public relations and editing the employee newsletter. I took pictures and wrote articles. But I didn't tell anybody on the job that I was a recovering alcoholic. I was "passing" as a regular person who just didn't drink.

Pretty quickly I learned that writing for an in-house publication is hardly what you'd call investigative reporting. Trying to beef up a Department of the Month article on the hospital switchboard, I asked the question, "Do the operators ever listen in?" Later, the assistant hospital administrator called me into his office for a chat about the purpose of such articles. Nothing negative, nothing deep, he said. Just fun stories.

I left the PR job after less than a year.

My next job was working in an ad agency for a couple who were friends of mine, writing copy for their hotel chain account. I was bad at it.

I couldn't figure out why I hated writing jobs so much when I was a writer.

A therapist I went to (he was also a best-selling writer) gave me the simple answer.

"There's writing and there's writing."

I was so relieved. It was okay not to get just any job as a writer. I could write only what I wanted to write on my own—and get a support-myself job doing something else. If he hadn't said that I might be struggling with ad slogans for cereal boxes by now.

When I told the company I was leaving, they understood. My boss even gave me a compliment.

"You have a marvelous attitude," he said.

Marvelous attitude! I'd never had such a grown-up compliment before. It felt good.

My love life was similarly unfocused.

I had no idea what I wanted in a man. So this was the other area where I had to find out what I liked by eliminating what I didn't like, the lemons and the doozies.

When I was six months sober I began to date an ex-priest who was also an ex-husband and had a son. I met him in a recovery group meeting where he had a reputation for slipping (not being able to stay off his drugs of choice), for being a liar and for chasing after newly sober women (like me) who were still too dazed to catch on to what he was up to.

During the entire six months I dated Joel, he was stoned on pills. I never knew it. I was oblivious when he drove on the wrong side of roads. I didn't notice when he fell asleep in strange places (taxis). I thought nothing of it when he told me he had to fly to Washington, D.C., to act as a consultant in a Russian spy case—all of which made me perfect for him.

Pauline was wise to Joel but on purpose she didn't tell me. She wanted me to find out for myself. Still, she hovered close.

"Call me any time of the day or night if you need to discuss how it's going with Joel," she said, none too subtly.

"You're saying I'm going to need to do that?"

"Not necessarily. Just that the kind of man you're likely to be attracted to now probably won't do a thing for you when you're a year sober."

About a week before I celebrated my first year of sobriety I told Joel goodbye. It wasn't that I smartened up. Just what I already knew was enough—his mood swings, his jealousy ("How do *I* know who you're meeting on your job?"), his chronic date cancelling. But I think the coup de grace was sexual. I stepped out of the shower one night and there were no towels. I called for Joel to bring me one. When I opened the bathroom door to get it, Joel averted his eyes. He felt uncomfortable seeing me naked—and we'd been sleeping together for months.

Deep in my gut I got a message that I didn't even want to get: this man hates women!

After that I didn't want him to touch me.

It was over.

The phone calls started immediately afterwards.

Ring.

"Hello?"

Click.

It was unnerving.

I knew it was Joel. Three in the morning, five at night (my witching hour), eight in the morning, noon. And this man had been a *priest*!

"Pauline, how could I have picked out such a fruitcake to fall for? What's *wrong* with me? How come I have such poor judgment and bad taste?"

"One, you were lonely. Two, you still lack self-worth."

"Three, I'm still an asshole!"

"Change your phone number."

"I can do that?"

"Are you a grown-up?"

I hesitated. "Yes!"

"Then you can do it!"

I did it.

A woman I knew in the recovery group suggested I look for work in the alcoholism field—as a psychotherapist. I had the right credentials, including my Marriage, Family and Child Counseling license, a desirable license in California.

I had a funny reaction: "No way!"

"No way?" she said. "Who do you think alcoholics *are*? *Us*! You and me and a lot of our friends."

"Oh." I'd never thought of it like that. The word "alcoholic" still brought those images of skid row bums to mind.

I decided to check it out. I volunteered at the National Council on Alcoholism—the place I'd turned myself in to so many sleeps ago. Ruth wasn't there anymore. I never ran across her again.

Ursula was the new secretary. She was a recovering alcoholic like me. Sometimes it seemed as if we were everywhere.

The first time she asked me to handle a help call, I froze.

"No, Ursula, I can't. I don't know enough about alcoholism yet. I haven't read any of the right books."

"You *are* an alcoholic, aren't you?"

"Yes."

"Then that's what you tell her."

"Tell her I'm an alcoholic? Are you crazy?"

It was all so contrary to my training back in Boston where I'd been taught that as a therapist I should stay out of the picture, be a blank screen onto which the patient could only project his or her own fantasies of what we were like. We shouldn't let the patient know if we were married, if we had opinions. And most definitely we shouldn't let the patient know we weren't perfect.

I figured that being an alcoholic might possibly be construed as not being perfect!

So by the time I took the phone from Ursula I was shaking in pure anticipation of the caller's reaction to what I was about to say:

"Hi, I'm Sylvia. I'm an alcoholic. Can I help you?"

When I hung up twenty minutes later, I realized that it had been a whole decade since I first became a psychotherapist back in Boston. And never once had I felt like a healer.

But today I did.

A few months later I ended up on skid row—I got a job there. It was in a detox and rehabilitation center.

At that time, about one hundred and twenty drunk arrests were made a day in the skid row area. Most of the drunks were thrown into jail for the night to sober up and then tossed back onto the streets the next day to get drunk again. Some had been through this process hundreds of times.

This was a small, new, private, two-story facility and its stated function was to step into this revolving door and save people.

A few dozen "clients" (a term giving instant status) lived at the detox center and over a period of months were not only detoxed and fed, but were clothed, vitamined, therapied, grouped (I led groups), social worked and vocationally guided. At nights they were taken to local meetings of Alcoholics Anonymous.

The brains behind this operation was a man named Red. The detox center was his baby.

Red was a sensuously handsome man with, of course, red hair and charm and the charisma of a cult leader.

And I was (I soon learned) a cultee just waiting to happen!

Red had utopian goals for the place, which of course would extend out and not only touch the community, but the world. There'd be dancing in the streets soon, the way he described it. And if there was one thing I was always a sucker for, it was Utopia. Damn, but I loved crusades! Originally, it was going to be Freud who'd save the world (everybody would be psychoanalyzed and happy and there'd be no more war). Then it was going to be the women's movement (everybody would be equal and happy and there'd be no more war). Now it was going to be Red (everybody would be sober and happy and there'd be no more war).

A few weeks later the atmosphere of the detox center began to change. Red began treating us more like kids than employees. He was Big Daddy. He'd be a scolding Big Daddy one minute and a hugging, tears-in-the-eyes, forgiving Big Daddy the next. He began to confront individual staff members over minor transgressions. But by the time Red got through ranting and raving, the transgressions seemed major, premeditated, and vile.

When a counselor named Curt forgot to pay two of the "clients" for washing his car, Red called a meeting and confronted Curt, accusing him of intentionally ripping off the clients. Initially Curt defended himself.

"Jesus, I just forgot!"

"That's bullshit! Am I right?"

He said "Am I right?" in such a way as to suggest that he was privy to private information that, if brought out, would prove for sure he was right.

"Am I?"

Curt wavered. Red went for the jugular and in no time had Curt and the rest of us believing that unconsciously Curt was a snob; that Curt had "forgotten" to pay the skid row bums because of a deep, underlying feeling of superiority; he didn't find them worthy of payment.

"And I don't know what the hell you think you have to be so superior about when from what I hear you can't even get it up anymore!" Red said. "Am I right?" Suddenly there was dead silence in the room.

After that, I became afraid of Red. I was afraid of another such meeting where someone else might have their secrets exposed. Whenever I walked past Red's office, I'd get nervous. Sometimes his door would be closed and behind it I'd hear Red shouting and then I'd hear someone crying. I'd scurry on down the hall as fast as I could and hide out.

Not once did it occur to me to mention what was going on to Pauline. Nor did I figure out that nobody should have to be afraid to go to work. I was now going there each day aware that when I stepped inside the building, the rules changed. The rules of the "outside" became irrelevant. Here, Red was the law.

The only person I dared talk to was Julian, a good-looking, street-wise Mexican ex-heroin addict who was a counselor trainee and had made enough under-the-breath comments about Red (like "bastard") for me to trust him.

I clung onto Julian. I got a crush on Julian and flirted with Julian to the point where it showed. A suicidal action around Red.

Red called me into his office late one afternoon.

When he shut the door I knew it was my turn.

"What's with you and Julian?"

"Nothing." I knew I shouldn't have said that the minute I did.

"Don't give me that!"

"I like him."

"Are you attracted to him?"

Maybe straight-on honesty would help me now: "Yes."

"Ah-HAH! So *that's* it!" I knew honesty was the wrong choice. "That's what turns you women's libbers on these days, isn't it—third worlders! Am I right?"

I said nothing. I was spacing out—something I did when I got confused.

154

"I suppose you get your jollies from leading a man like that on and then when he's hot, telling him to go screw off, am I right?"

I could see we were off to the races. And I could see it starting—the self-doubt. *Was* he right?

Red kept talking. He stood. I sat, looking up at him. He was painting a picture, the picture of a white, economically advantaged seductress coldly taking advantage of an underprivileged and helpless Mexican. Just listening to Red I began to hate this woman myself. Is that who I really was? Was he seeing something in me I couldn't see? *Was* he right?

"Tomorrow I'm calling a meeting to discuss staff relationships," Red said.

I began to cry.


On the freeway going home that night I followed a line of thinking that seemed rational, logical. Sobriety hadn't uncovered a good person in me after all. Sobriety had uncovered an evil person in me who'd toy with the downtrodden—like Julian. And it took Red, who was a truly brilliant and maybe special person, to see it. Therefore it followed, as the night follows the day, that I should remove myself from the people I love and who love me so as not to contaminate them with my inherent evil nature. Therefore, I should *die*.

I was thinking from the bottom of my geek pit and I didn't even realize I was back there.


When I got home I called Pauline, a routine "check in." I didn't even bother to mention work. It didn't seem that important. Besides, I knew she'd judge it all by outside standards and outside standards couldn't be applied here. So it was easier to skip it.

But then Pauline asked, "How's work?"

"Okay."

"Just okay?"

"There's a staff meeting tomorrow I'm a little worried about. Other than that okay."

I wanted to get off the subject.

"What about it worries you?" Pauline was pushy at times.

"Nothing special. It's just that it's my turn on the hot seat, I guess."

"Explain that to me."

I told her in a sketchy way the events of the afternoon, including my visit to Red's office.

"Run that by me again. Red said *what* to you about Julian?" I could feel the hairs on the back of her neck standing up. I reacted by actually defending Red.

"He can be very nice at times, Pauline, and he's got exciting plans for the place."

"He's a lunatic," she said. "Get out of there right away."

"You mean quit my job!"

"Yes, I do."

Strange relief overcame me.

"Shouldn't I tough it out for a while, show I can take it now that I'm sober? Don't I have a responsibility to show my employer that recovering alcoholics are even better employees than regular people? Shouldn't I at least try?"

"No."

More relief. "Okay. Tomorrow I'll give my two weeks' notice."

"No, tomorrow you're *out* of there."

"I can *do* that?"

"Would you give two weeks' notice to leave a burning building?"

"No."

"Is he worth drinking over?"

"No."

"Then quit. If you don't, you'll drink. I can see it coming. You've already had thoughts about killing yourself, am I right?"

She sounded like Red! And how did she *know* that? I was too stunned to answer. She read my mind.

"I know that because you're a sober alcoholic and you want to stay sober; otherwise you'd have thought of drinking before suicide. I think it's great. It shows me you're committed, so you get out of that place and you're going to be okay."

"And you're sure it's okay not to give two weeks' notice?"

I could see my tombstone now: "Here Lies Sylvia. She Did The Right Thing. She Gave Two Weeks' Notice."

"Yes I'm sure."

"Okay," I said.

I drove to skid row the next morning with my letter of resignation to give to Red personally, eyeball to eyeball. I still felt the need to do something "strong."

Shaking, I climbed the flight of stairs towards Red's office only to find that his door was closed and there was shouting coming from it—and I heard crying.

At that point I slid the envelope under Red's door and ran like hell.

# – 24 –

# GOODBYE TO WALT

*Love is letting people be who they are
—and who they are not.*

—*Werner Erhard*

Sobriety helps people join the human race, not transcend it. Sober we get to handle the things that other people have been out there handling all along, the good stuff as well as the bad stuff.

When I'd been sober a year (everything was now measured time in terms of sobriety—either "Before I got sober..." or "After I got sober...") I flew to New York with Emily and Abby for my sister's wedding. Justine was marrying a tall, chatty, warm man named Robert whom she'd met in law school.

During the flight I wouldn't leave my seat, move too fast or talk for fear I'd make the plane fall down.

Before Sobriety (B.S.) martinis and Valiums kept planes up for me. But now I couldn't have those things so flying was miserable. Here I was working so hard on becoming A Better Person with emotional courage—and I'd gone and lost my physical courage.

When Pauline gave me one of her "If-you're-meant-to-die-you'll-die-no-matter-where-you-are" pep talks at the airport, I snapped at her, "Shut up, Pauline!"

There was a cloud over this wedding because of my stepfather Walt's impending surgery for what looked like throat cancer—*his* biggest fear. His own father had died of it only five years earlier.

Walt's condition had been complicated by self-medication—doses of either vodka and orange juice, or Scotch and milk, throughout the day. Walt was a "buzz-on" drinker. He maintained a buzz-on all day long. He was never really drunk. But he was never sober either. There was always that veil between him and the rest of us.

"He had one of his fall-aparts the week of my bar exams," Justine told me on the way back to Connecticut from the airport in New York. "I was furious at him. It was like he was doing it on purpose just to stop me from taking the bar. He was crying, begging me not to leave him—God knows why—but dammit I wasn't going to let him do that to me. I knew I'd resent him forever if I let him keep me here, so I got a train back to New York and I didn't even call Mom to see how he was doing until after the bar. By the way, all that Alanon literature you sent about dealing with alcoholics was so helpful. Thanks."

She had, of course, passed the bar—my little sister, little Justine "Justice." How I used to boss her around when we were kids. I made her so mad sometimes she'd be forced to seek immediate justice by biting me. Now here she was, a *criminal* lawyer. I gave her a big hug. It was good to see her. I loved her spunk, and how well she took care of herself. She'd never had to go through alcoholism or fall on her face to learn how to cope—she just coped.

Abby, now seven, was so much like her. She and Justine had spent little time together, yet they sounded alike and often had similar expressions on their faces. But Abby was beginning to display a new trait that Justine had never developed: "Mom, how come Justine has whitish yellow light around her head," she casually asked me one afternoon, "but Grandpa Walt has a brownish one that's thinnish like he has no energy?"

"My God! You see auras!" I said. "That's fabulous!" If she'd said that here a few hundred years earlier she'd have been burned as a witch.

"What's auras?"

After a few days in Connecticut I got a bee in my bonnet. I'd been saved from demon rum and now Walt would have to be saved.

And I was the one who was going to save him.

"Daddy, please go to a recovery group meeting with me."

Walt didn't want to be saved. "Leave me alone, Sylvie-Sylvie. Scoot!"

"It's not what you think. It's not skid row bums."

"I know what it's like. I did a piece on recovery groups once. And it's not for me. I don't like groups, and don't want to go."

We began to bicker about things, little things—the shortest route to the market, which burner to use for boiling water, how many hours

158

ahead of us Dusseldorf was—things Walt used to call "ascertainable facts"—things that could be looked up. Back in high school if I'd say, "London is *not* north of Liverpool, it's *west* of Liverpool," Walt would say, "That's an ascertainable fact," meaning we weren't allowed to discuss it further at the dinner table.

"Did you *see* how much Scotch Daddy put in his milk this morning?" I said to my mother a few days later. My thirst for drama had returned.

"'To watch is not to love,'" she said. She must have gotten that from the Alanon literature.

"He's so *sneaky* about it," I said.

"And you're so judgmental about it."

I phoned Pauline in Los Angeles.

"My stepfather seems so pissed off at me all the time," I complained, "and I'm only trying to help him."

"First of all, your sobriety is a threat to him. It's making him look at his own drinking and he's not ready to do that. He's got other things on his mind, like maybe dying."

"But if he's got throat cancer, drinking is the *last* thing he should be doing!"

"Did you stop drinking when you found out it was bad for you?"

"No."

"Then stop judging him and love him exactly the way he is."

Later that afternoon when I was washing dishes I looked out the window over the sink onto the screened porch. There was Walt, sitting at the table, gazing out over his beloved "estate." He didn't know he was being watched.

I thought of bits and pieces of our past together, how excited I was (I was Abby's age, seven) when this handsome man married my mother and did the tango with her in our living room on their wedding night. On the way to the wedding supper in a French restaurant, I held his hand as we walked down Lexington Avenue. I made my mother walk behind so people would say, "Oh, there's a little girl with her *daddy!*" I remembered how my first tantrum scared him into tears (he got used to them); how he'd be the daddy to pick me up at parties and take other kids home; how he made sure I got my teeth cleaned; how he'd swing me around ("airplane rides"—I wasn't phobic then!). He had tin boxes full of treasure-junk and once, snooping in desk drawers, I found a picture of his first wife, a dancer named Wanda, holding huge bare tits with erect nipples pointed right at the camera lens. Quickly I put the picture back under other things.

Did he ever think of Wanda now?

Sometimes I did badly in school; sometimes I did well in school—but either way, Walt always told me I was beautiful, told me that he was proud of his "Sylvie-Sylvie," said over and over that he loved me.

Walt had loved me—unconditionally—just as I was.

I dried my hands, walked out onto the screened porch, went up to Walt, stood next to him in his chair and put my arms around him.

He responded immediately, almost gratefully. He put his arms around my hips and leaned his head into my stomach, like a small child. "My beautiful Sylvie-Sylvie," he said. "I do love you so very much."

I stroked his head, feeling that same love feeling I had that night for my children when Pauline had made me stay home and be with them alone.

"I love you too, Daddy."

We held each other silently.

It was our last private moment together.

Later in the day sitting with Justine and Robert in the living-room, I heard Walt in the kitchen pouring a drink. Next I saw him through the front window, glass in hand, strolling along the edges of the lawn.

Justine saw him too. She turned to me with tears in her eyes and she gave me a sad little smile.

"Estate-walking," she said.

Walt was operated on a few weeks after the wedding. It was throat cancer. At first I was happy they hadn't torn his voice out and left him with a hole, but later on I understood why; it was too late.

He went home from the hospital, then back again a few months later where he had an alcoholic convulsion on the operating table and died.

Walt had died not of cancer, but of alcoholism!

It devastated me.

"He'd be alive now if he'd stopped drinking—at least for a while!" I said to Pauline when I got back from his funeral. "Why didn't he listen to me? *Other* people get to help their parents stop drinking, why couldn't I?"

"I can't answer that," Pauline said sympathetically. "I wish I could."

"I *hate* alcoholism! I hate what it does to people! Most people have no idea how awful it is. I just hate it!"

"They say that some people have to die so that others may live," Pauline said.

I wrote a query letter for an article idea I had on the subject of alcoholism and began sending it out to national magazines. Walt's death made me want to communicate things about this illness that had snatched him away from me too fast and had nearly done me in too. When one of the magazines came right out and told me in print that they couldn't run an article on alcoholism because they carried too many liquor ads, I was furious—and more determined.

Finally my drinking and recovery story appeared in *Ms.* magazine with just my first name and last initial. I thought I was keeping a low profile, but people in my past life came out of the woodwork and wrote me—people I was sure had either forgotten me or, worse, hated me.

"So *that's* where you've been all these years!" an old work supervisor from Boston wrote me via *Ms.* magazine. "We were so glad to find you and so sorry to hear about all you've been through. But it sounds like you're okay now which is wonderful. Please get in touch and drop in for a visit next time you're back in Boston."

When I read this and other such mail, I cried.

Maybe I wasn't such a terrible person after all.

A few months after the article appeared in *Ms.*, I spoke at a meeting of my recovery group. As usual, I simply told my story—what it was like when I was drinking, what happened to get me to stop, and what my life was like now that I was sober. I'd followed the same format in my article.

Right after the meeting a tall young woman in a business suit came over to me, eyes luminous.

"My God, you're the Sylvia who wrote the *Ms.* article! I can't believe it—*you're* why I'm here! When I read that article I realized for the first time I was an alcoholic and I've been sober ever since. I was sitting here thinking, hmm, this lady's story sounds so familiar—and then I realized!"

She gave me a hug. "Thank you!"

I flashed on what Pauline had said about some people having to die so that others may live.

Walt had died. His death made me mad. I wrote the article for *Ms.* about alcoholism. This woman read it—and here she was.

# – 25 –

# GOODBYE TO MOM

*Throughout the whole of life one must continue to learn
to live, and what will amaze you even more, throughout life
one must learn to die.*

—*Seneca, quoted by Scott Peck, M.D.*
The Road Less Traveled

My next job was a far cry from skid row. It was working with "silk
sheet" drunks and addicts at a private chemical dependency hospital.
It was a good job in a supportive environment. I was no longer afraid
to go to work.

The problem was getting there—it was far away, over an hour on
the freeway each way.

For a couple of months I tried to handle everything—getting the
girls to school, commuting, picking the girls up at the daycare center,
Emily's Gestalt therapy, dance lessons, grocery shopping, cooking
dinner, laundry and cleaning, then getting to a recovery group meeting
and when I could, a date.

I was a wreck.

This wasn't at all what I had in mind when I'd picketed for the
"right" to work! This was exhausting. But I'd fought so hard for my
right to be exhausted that I didn't dare complain! Besides, I assumed
I was having a hard time because I was inadequate, not because I was
doing too much. It would be a few more years before those articles
on the Superwoman Syndrome would begin to appear and name the
problem.

I just thought I was a flop.

"Don't cut back on your meetings," Pauline kept telling me. "Most
people who drink again do it because they stop going to meetings."

I was snappish. "I'm too tired! Try *my* schedule for a week and see how it feels!" I wanted to throw some things in her face, like how *she* had it easy—no children (she couldn't have any), no job she had to show up for and a nice husband to support her so she could sit around on her ass all day and give other people advice about working!

Fortunately, I kept my mouth shut.


One Friday when Sandy came to pick up the girls and I was lying on the couch with the freeway still zinging in my ears, I asked his guidance. What should I do about the job? Should I move closer to work? Should I send the girls to boarding school? Should I hire a nurse? If I did, could he help me pay for it? Should I quit? What?

Sandy heard me out. Then he said: "I'll take them."

"You? You mean have them live with you?"

"Sure. I'd like it."

"No."

"Why not?"

"I just can't do that."

"Why not?"

I didn't know why not. All I knew was the very idea scared me. What would people think? It wasn't "in" yet for children to live with daddies instead of mommies. The only time children lived with daddies was when mommies were drunkies or were promiscuous or maybe psychotic.

I didn't want anyone speculating about which of those things *I* was.

"No." I'll send them to boarding school first!

"Think about it," Sandy said.

"I'll think about thinking about it."

"Fine. Whatever."


"Pauline! Pauline, it's me, Sylvia! Can you hear me? I've got a problem!" I was shouting into the phone and it was coming out into Pauline's big kitchen through the squawk box she'd just had installed so she could cook dinner and save lives at the same time.

"I'm listening, hon," she shouted back. "I'm washing lettuce but I can hear you just fine."

"Pauline, I'm thinking of giving my kids away."

There was a silence.

"To Goodwill?"

I caught a funny edge to her voice. It made me shiver.

"No, to Sandy. He offered."

"I see."

"I don't know what else to do. I need to get my work act together if I'm going to be able to support myself once the alimony stops. And I can't do it and handle the kids too. I need to be able to concentrate. I need to be able to get to work on time and stay late if I have to. I need to begin taking my work seriously for once. Do you understand?"

"I think you should do whatever makes you comfortable, dear, you know that. Whatever you choose, you have my blessing."

Why did I feel as though she'd just said "fuck you!"?

"Pauline?"

"Yes, I'm listening. Here, I'll even turn the water off."

She did. Now it was easier to talk.

"Pauline, are you by any chance judging me?"

Dead silence.

Then she said, simply, "Yes."

"But *why?*" I felt so guilty anyway and to have her displeased with me on top of it felt like more than I could bear.

"I think it's because I envy your having children," she said. "I don't understand not wanting to live with them."

Now I was getting more upset by the second.

"You always tell *me* not to be judgmental!" I wailed.

"Yes, I do. And judgmentalness is one of *my* character defects too. How do you think I recognize it in you?"

"But you're not *supposed* to be judgmental!" I could hear anger in my voice, indignation—but not the righteous kind. Just a plain tantrum. "You're my mentor. You're supposed to have your act together! You're supposed to be—"

"Perfect?"

In a very weak little voice I said, "Yes."

Then I started to cry. I wept like a scared little girl. "Pauline, why am I crying? I don't understand. I can't seem to stop!"

"You're crying because you're disappointed in me. You've just found out I'm human and have limitations and you don't like it. And Sylvia, you should know that human beings will *always* fail you, no matter who they are."

"That sounds so cynical."

"Maybe, but it's the truth. That's why we need to find a non-human power to depend on that won't fail us, an inner power or—and I know you hate to hear this—a higher power."

This was draining me. I had no fight left, no answers, no energy to "mouth off about that God shit" the way I usually did. All I could do was weep and picture my weeping coming into Pauline's country kitchen through the squawk box, getting into her cakes, into her salad, into her meat loaf. She and John would eat my sobs for supper and be full of them for days.

"Before we hang up, I need to make amends for my judgmentalness," Pauline said. "You showed me I still have some work to do on myself in that area!"

"But what do I do about the kids?"

"I meant what I said. It has to be your decision. And if you make the wrong one, you can always make another decision down the line. Sometimes knowing that helps. There'll be a price to pay either way. Every decision has a price tag. So just pick the one with the price you're most willing to pay. And please know that I'll still love you either way."

Sigh of relief.

"And I'd like you to talk to a friend of mine, Rochelle. She shipped her four kids back to live with her ex-husband for a couple of years and it worked out just fine. Call her. It might make you feel better."

Aside from her choice of the word "shipped," I was grateful for the suggestion. "Thanks."

I hung up and dialed Rochelle.

After that, for the first time in my sobriety, I struggled with a major decision on my own.

What I decided was to accept Sandy's offer.

I phoned him: "How's it going?" I asked.

"Everything is falling apart, but I'm fine."

Everything *was* falling apart. At forty-two he "had" to get married! His pretty blond twice-married girlfriend, Kathy, got pregnant and wouldn't have an abortion. She had three other kids. In her eighth month Sandy agreed to get married to give the baby a name but he refused to live with her. Business as usual.

"I'm a loner. Loners like to live alone."

"Did I do that to you? Poison you about marriage?"

"You helped."

When baby Brian arrived, Sandy adored him and there were plenty of visits back and forth between the two houses—but still no living together.

Kathy pushed at him to change his mind, but Sandy doesn't push. I was surprised she hadn't learned that.

The more she pushed, the more he resisted.

They started having fights. Kathy was a screamer and a door-slammer.

"Are you still up to taking on the girls?" I said.

"Sure, why not?"

"Even though you're a loner?"

"It's adult company I don't like."

"Are you sure you can cope with it?"

"No."

"Do you know how to do laundry? Can you cook?"

You would have thought I was hiring an *au pair*.

I pressed on. "What if one of them gets sick?"

"I'll call a doctor."

I forgot he *was* a doctor!

"Will you remember to pick them up at six from the daycare center?"

"Most of the time."

"Come on, Sandy, I'm serious!"

Emily, as usual, went along with the move to Sandy's without a whimper. It was as though she was oblivious to things going on in the world around her—or she didn't care. Or she cared *too* much. There was simply no way to tell. She gave no clues.

Abby, on the other hand, cried.

It broke my heart!

I'd been teaching her to tell the truth about her feelings, but now that she was doing that I hated it. It made me feel so guilty! Why couldn't she just say, "Yes, Mommy dear" and get an ulcer!

"I'll miss you, Mommy!"

"It's only ten minutes away."

"It's not the same!"

"You'll see me weekends."

"It's still not the same! I want to live here! PLEASE!"

I ran out of the room. Oh, God, what was I doing? I was full of doubts and self-recriminations. I was a bad mother! I was hurting my children!

This was the one time I knew I couldn't call Pauline.

I was in this one alone.

We survived—all of us.

167

Abby, as usual, bounced back and was once again happy.

Emily drifted along as though nothing had happened.

And for a spell even Kathy settled down and did a lot of crafts and baking now that there were six kids in the picture.

I thought it was kind of funny, a loner like Sandy ending up with two wives and six children!

Sandy did a good job as a father. I was impressed.

Childcare for him, being a man, wasn't a loaded issue the way it was for me. When he had to stay home with a sick child it wasn't demeaning. When he had to wait in the pediatrician's office he didn't look upon it as part of a conspiracy to keep him away from his work the way I did. In fact, he was glad for the chance to sit down and read *Time* magazine.

To Sandy, childcare was just another responsibility on his list: new tires; prepare notes for hypnosis seminar; make dentist appointment for Emily; bill insurance company, etc. It was all the same.

At Christmas my blue-eyed mother Bonnie, lonely now in the big Connecticut house without Walt, came to California for a three-week visit.

She'd gained a little weight. "The widow is overeating," she said. "I've joined a gym."

Other than that, she made no reference to her loss or her pain. She put all her energies into Emily and Abby—and into trying to get me to move them back in with me.

She was, as usual, worried sick about Emily who was now ten.

"She's so hauntingly beautiful, so vulnerable. What will become of her? How will she fend for herself? How will she live?"

"I don't know yet. There's nothing more I can do. She's in special education classes at school. She goes to therapy. She's not unhappy, really, she's okay."

"She *needs* you, Sylvie."

"Drop it, please!"

I took my mother to one of my recovery meetings. She wasn't comfortable.

"I can understand something like that for some people, Sylvie, but for people like us, don't you think we need something a little more sophisticated, something with a little depth to it, like therapy?"

"Jesus Christ, this group saved my life! Isn't that 'depth' enough?"

I was relieved when she flew back to Connecticut.

Four months later she was dead too.

A cerebral hemorrhage got her one day while she was busy at her typewriter working on a book.

Gratefully, she didn't die right away and I had a chance to fly to Connecticut and be with her for eight days and repair some of the damage I felt had been done by that tense Christmas visit.

In good spirits, she was sure she was on the mend. So was I.

"I apologize," I said.

"For what, Sylvie?"

"For taking so long to grow up."

The night I got back to Los Angeles from her funeral I went to a recovery meeting to get grounded. I was very uptight. At the meeting I heard a woman talking about priorities.

"If it's alive, it's a priority."

The phrase stuck.

I realized that I'd had it backwards.

I'd spent years focusing on work, work, work.

Now it was time to focus in on people.

# – 26 –

# ELEPHANT CHIPPING

*If you have not lived through something, it is not true.*
—*Kabir, 16th Century Sufi*

Over the next several years I threw myself into the world of self-improvement. I joined the Find Out Who I Am And Become A Better Person movement. I called it elephant-chipping, after the old Buddhist story about the sculptor who completes a statue of an elephant in his backyard and invites a friend over to see it. The friend is impressed: "That's great. How did you do it?" "Oh, that's easy," says the sculptor. "I just chipped away everything that wasn't an elephant."

That's what I was doing—chipping away everything that wasn't Sylvia.

Like an adrenaline addict, I spun through workshops, weekends, groups, classes, lectures and therapies like the Tasmanian devil. I joined a Nichirin Shoshu Buddhist temple and learned to meditate and chant, trying to find that non-human power Pauline kept nagging me about...I listened to Ram Dass tapes...I read Krishnamurti...I got a crush on the man who took me to hear Krishnamurti speak, but the man was only interested in taking me to hear Krishnamurti, just like he said he was...I went to the Bodhi Tree Bookstore and drank herb tea and bought musk oil and even a book...I went to Science of Mind...I took the est training...I floated in float tanks...I got my orange belt in karate...I had three years of training at the Gestalt Therapy Institute and found out I didn't want to be a Gestalt therapist...I jogged...I joined Jack LaLanne...I took a course in stained-glass window-making...I took screenwriting classes...I took Spanish...I took French at

UCLA...I got my thighs pounded...I was acupunctured for my back problem...I was hypnotized for my plane phobia...I was clonked on the head with a peacock feather by the guru Muktananda. (I checked him out after interviewing an actress for Canadian *TV Guide*. She told me that he'd shown her the light.)...I stopped eating red meat...I stopped smoking...I started smoking...I stopped smoking again (helped along by another "flash experience")...I stopped eating sugar...I *started* eating sugar again (I'm *still* eating sugar!)...I bought a cabin in the Idyllwild woods with the money my mother left me (and took the kids there on weekends)...I bought a camper with the rest of the money that my mother left me (and took the kids on a cross-country trip)...I went to work for the National Council on Alcoholism (again), doing PR (again), where I attempted to make alcoholism into a "chic" disease (Let's bury that stigma, folks!)...I sold my cabin when I ran out of money...I quit the National Council after a couple of years to write a book...I ran out of money before I could finish the book and went back to work. When my poor employer looked at my resume he said, rather nervously, "You've moved around a bit." (Later I left him, too!)...And I left the next employer too when he turned out to be another Red. Only this time I got to give my two weeks' notice.

"You know, watching you is like watching a light show," Sandy commented to me one day.

"I'm still elephant-chipping," I said. "The only way I know how to find out what I want is by eliminating everything I *don't* want."

"There must be a better way."

"Tell me and I'll try that, too."

The girls were back living with me again. We'd moved away from the beach to a little house in Brentwood with a big Connecticut backyard and trees. I'd decided I wasn't a beach person, I was a tree person. Another elephant chip.

Abby seemed to get a kick out of my being a Mom-in-Motion. "You're *into* things," she said. "I like that. I like it when my friends ask me, 'What's your Mom into now?' I hope I'm like you when I grow up."

"I appreciate your interpretation of it," I said.

It looked like the only two things that I was doing consistently in my life were staying single and staying sober—and oh, God, was I tired of staying single.

I'd put all those years into improving myself; I'd done all that work figuring out my top ten "Musts" in a man only to discover that I'd sailed past forty and there weren't any.

What a shock!

Here I'd gotten my act together and they'd closed the theater! Here I'd decided I was the faithful type and I couldn't even find anyone to be faithful to, let alone unfaithful with.

I felt like the fussy spinster who woke up on the morning of her seventy-eighth birthday and said: "By God, I've got it! What I've been wanting all along is a beach boy!"

And it was too late.

Now I'd been sobered, weathered and made wiser; now that I was ripe to get married, the universe was saying, "Big Deal!"

That's when the active man-hunting years began (although one must never admit one is on such a quest; I said things like "I'm joining Desperate Singles to meet interesting people.")

I stalked the surround like a lioness looking for food. I was looking for Him.

My new no-nonsense mentor, Inez (Pauline broke my heart by moving away) didn't approve.

"You shouldn't go looking for a man. Men appear when you're not looking for them."

So I tried not looking, which was like trying not to think of peanuts. I'd sit at a meeting and find myself surveying the audience row-by-row, up one row and down the other, making a decision about each man: No...no...no...hmm?...no...no...maybe, but probably no...taken... no...yich!...no, etc. Then I'd catch myself. Sylvia, you're not supposed to be looking!

Even when I was too tired to look, I looked. Evenings I'd have preferred to stay home and be cozy, I'd feel that lioness pressure to go hunting. If you don't go, Sylvia, you might miss something. This might be the night He is there.

Once in a while I'd pounce and ask a man out for coffee.

"Let the man ask *you* out for coffee," Inez would say.

"What is this you're telling me, Inez? It's archaic!" Inez had been married forever. I was skeptical that she had any idea what the relationship scene was like these days. "Do you know what the odds are for a woman my age finding a man? It's probably about twenty of us to one of them."

"Are you sure those aren't the odds for princes?"

173

"Men are scarce."

"All you need is one. Maybe you're putting out the wrong vibes, Sylvia. Did you ever think of that?"

"Who, *me*? Impossible!"

A week later I had my camper parked at a meter in Santa Monica. When I returned to it, a handsome, well-dressed man was standing next to it, looking in.

"I was admiring your camper."

"Oh, let me show it off to you."

I opened up the sliding side door and proceeded to dazzle him with the camper's features: built-in toilet, CB radio, stove, refrigerator, sink with running water, supplies. I told him I could read maps, pump gas, change tires, cook over a fire and fend off banditos. (Hadn't I taken karate?)

When I finished, he bowed—actually bowed—just like a real prince.

"Your camper is very good-looking and very self-contained," he said, "just like its owner." And he walked away.

Walked away!

"You're right!" I wailed to Inez. "I did my superwoman number on him! I wanted him to know I wouldn't be too much trouble."

"Next time, just be yourself."

"Great. Who is that?"

I turned in my camper for a helpless-looking little black sedan with wire wheels and tinted windows.

It's not that there were *no* men. But there were none I wanted to marry (even if they'd asked!).

"You women are too fussy, you want everything all rolled into one," a therapist (male) said.

"Isn't that the truth. And rape is our fault, too."

But of course what I thought was: He's right. I'll try compromise.

My first Compromise was a man who had all the right traits except one—there was no chemistry. Whenever he kissed me, instead of feeling aroused, I felt rage.

Then there was the Compromise who was overly sensitive and wimpy. He was so intimidated by me that whenever I walked into a room he'd literally jump backwards to make way for me. It infuriated me.

174

Then there was the Compromise who wore army boots and walked like a demolition crew across a room. Bang! Bang! Five minutes into our first date I screamed: "Shut up!"

After the Compromises came the Obsessions—men I just *knew* were perfect for me and vice versa, if only I could get them to stop withholding from me long enough to let me prove it to them. These were the ones whose evey kind word or thoughtful gesture I grossly misinterpreted: "But he sent me three whole postcards from his European vacation; he *must* care."

The Obsessions were the closest thing to drinking that I'd experienced since I'd been sober.

"God, they don't even get gradually better! One's as bad as the last or worse!" I complained to a college friend who'd just done the impossible: Married again. "Is it *me*? What am I doing wrong?"

"Just hang in there and it'll happen."

"And when the right one comes along I'll know, is that it?" I was being sarcastic.

"I hate to tell you this, but yes."

"Husband hunting is a numbers game, just like headhunting is," said a friend in the executive search field. "In the headhunting business the formula is forty calls a day gets you two home phone interviews a night. Two home phone interviews gets you two job interviews a month. Two job interviews a week gets you two placements a month. Your commission on two placements a month is between five and ten thousand dollars. Not too shabby. Strictly a numbers game."

"That's an awful lot of men, Pat."

"I think maybe I should have a game plan," I said to Inez. "What should I be looking for going in?"

"A man should have a healthy mind, a healthy body and a healthy pocketbook. That's what you should be looking for."

I found two just like that.

"They just *happen* to be married," I said to Inez defensively.

"'Happen' bullshit!" Inez didn't have Pauline's gentleness with me.

"Well, maybe it's better than having nothing."

"*Is* it?"

I thought about that a minute. "No."

After that I tried having nothing for a while. I needed the rest.

Sandy divorced Kathy. He was beginning to look like the only prince I'd ever known.

"Would you consider marrying me again?"

"No."

"Reason?"

"You're a friend. I don't have any friends. I need a friend more than a wife."

"So I should give up on that fantasy and get on with my life?"

"Sounds like a good idea."

During these years Harlan Yates, my Eskimo, kept popping up again and again. Usually I'd run into him in the Bank of America about once a year. It was like the play "Same Time, Next Year." The first year he looked like a hippy (he'd quit the stop-smoking business and was working for the nuclear freeze). The next year he looked conservative (he had a job as a social worker). Hmmm? Husband material? But the third year he looked hungover (he was drinking more). The fourth year he looked hyper (he was using cocaine). The fifth year he looked prosperous (he was dealing cocaine). He flashed a roll of bills and gave me three kinds of business cards: "I couldn't decide which design to have printed, so I had them *all* printed."

That was the year he asked me out to dinner.

I told him about being an alcoholic and about my recovery group as he ordered drink after drink and drank them down fast. I wanted to say "Don't gulp," but bit my tongue.

"One of these days I'm going to ask you to take me to a meeting," he said.

My experience with Walt had cured me of trying to fix people. All I could do was "carry the message."

"Sure," I said.

By the time we finished dinner (I ate—he didn't. Now I knew what that felt like! What goes out comes round!) Harlan was too drunk to drive home. I drove and made him come into my house and sleep it off on the beanbag in the middle of my living room. (The girls were at Sandy's.) For an hour I stroked his head, as if he were a little boy. At one point he woke up and his male ego asked me to go to bed with him. When I said no, he seemed relieved and fell right back to sleep.

"I'm serious about calling you to take me to a meeting," he said the next morning as he left.

"Sure."

A year later he did call and I did take him to a meeting. He found fault. He was cynical. But for a split second the speaker touched him and Harlan got tears in his eyes.

"Christ! That guy just zapped me for sure!"

But that was all he let in.

And *this* was the man who'd taught me all about feelings! Now alcohol and cocaine had anesthetized him. How I hated chemicals for snuffing out the beauty that used to be Harlan Yates. Harlan had been my "Eskimo guide." Why couldn't I be his?

But I had to give up on that one.

One day the following year I got home from work (whatever work I was into that season) and there was a message from Harlan on my answering machine: "Just want to let you know that this week I celebrate a year of being clean and sober. Thank you for your help. Maybe I'll see you at a meeting one of these days."

It wasn't quite like getting engaged, but it felt good.

# – 27 –

# THE FRUIT OF THE POISONED TREE

*I was angry with my friend:*
*I told my wrath, my wrath did end.*
*I was angry with my foe:*
*I told it not, my wrath did grow.*
 —*William Blake*
 *"A Poison Tree"*

The most dangerous emotion for the sober alcoholic is resentment—
because the best cure for resentment is gin.

Other people can churn about things and maybe get away with just
an ulcer, but alcoholics can't. For us, resentment = gin = death.

We simply can't afford the luxury of a grudge.

My resentment against my real father, Boo, went back years and
years. I was four when he left us, eleven when he began his country-hop-
ping, and twenty before I saw him again.

"I'm five feet three, have shoulder length dark brown hair, grey-blue
eyes and I'll be wearing a pink shirtdress," I'd had to tell him on the
phone after we'd arranged to meet again.

Boo got mad at America when he stopped writing well. He moved
to Italy, Mexico, Denmark, Greenland, and now Canada just to show
us all he didn't need us. In Italy, Denmark, and Canada he'd found
wives. I'd hear from him on alternate birthdays and occasional Christ-
mases.

It was all *great* resentment material, and I milked it. I told shrinks,
I told dates, I told husbands, I told friends, "And to top it off the
S.O.B. never sent us a dime. My mother sent *him* alimony." (Boo
was always good at getting women to sponsor his writing.)

The only person I never mentioned my resentment to was Boo himself.

When my mother died, I sent Boo a telegram in Quebec. His response was a punch in the gut. Instead of the sympathetic little note I'd expected, he wrote twenty pages of fury against my mother, against *her* mother (the poor woman had been dead thirty-four years) and against me for being a "lush" (I'd sent him my article in Ms. magazine) and even worse, for being "bourgeois."

I was crushed.

"If you go to an empty well for water that's what you have to expect," Inez had told me at the time. "You know what he's like."

I did. But it hurt anyway and caused a flare up in those geeky feelings that told me I wasn't worthy of life. Amazing how those thoughts could lie dormant for years and then, given the proper trigger, pop out in full force. I'd be walking around thinking I'd finally "arrived" at mental health—and the BAM! Back in the geek pit!

Inez understood. In her thirty years of sobriety she'd seen it all. "At the *core* of every alcoholic I've ever known lurks a feeling of low self-worth. I don't know why."

"But what do I *do*, Inez? *Now*?"

"Acknowledge that you're having an 'unworthy' attack and don't let it throw you."

"Yes, Inez." When I was hurting, I was very cooperative.

"And, Sylvia?"

"What?"

"One of these days you're going to have to handle your resentment about your father head on."

"I'm disowning him!"

"I didn't say now. I said someday."

It was spring and since early winter I'd been experiencing an increasing feeling of urgency to see Boo again. I wanted him to see the girls. He'd seen Emily once when she was a year old. He'd never seen Abby. I wanted them to meet him—"before it's too late" was the thought that kept occurring to me.

I'd be driving down Wilshire Boulevard, and suddenly I'd get visual pictures in my head of New England and I'd want to be there. Or I'd "see" Quebec (Sandy and I had been to Quebec together) and I'd want to be there.

So much so that I was having trouble concentrating on being in Los Angeles.

Finally I gave in.

I quit yet another job and when school was out, Emily, Abby and Mom-in-Motion took off across America one more time. My new license plate on my little black car was: "SEEKER 1."

Of course, I'd written Boo that we were coming. He'd written back: "Fine." Neither of us mentioned his nasty last letter or the fact that a few years of silence had set in as a result.

We took our time, stopping in New York and Connecticut to visit with Justine and Robert and their son and little daughter. We drove to Boston to see Mrs. Owens. And finally we began to wind our way north to Canada.

The day before we were to arrive in Quebec, I called Boo at his old folks' home.

He wasn't there.

The night before he'd been admitted to a hospital. Tests had been done. Bad news. Lung cancer. Inoperable. Terminal.

Our visit was just in time.

We found a motel and went right to the hospital.

Standing in the doorway of Boo's room I paused to absorb the shock of how small, how old and frail he looked. Boo stared at us blankly, not knowing at first who we were. Then suddenly the dawn broke. He grinned broadly.

"I'll be goddamned! I never really thought you'd come to visit an old fart like me!"

He opened his arms towards the girls. Emily and Abby both looked up at me to see if it was all right to go to him—they'd heard monster stories. I nodded and they went over to the side of Boo's bed and took turns hugging him.

"Hi, Boo," said Abby. I could tell the sick smells bothered her.

"Hi, Boo," said Emily, the echo.

Boo clapped his thin hands together. "Ah, how lovely they are! How graceful! What *pretty* little voices."

"God, Mom, I thought you said he was so terrible," Abby said to me later. "He's just an old man. I think he's nice."

Every morning the three of us went to see Boo in the hospital and every morning Boo refused his pain medication just so he could talk to us without being groggy. At least once per visit he'd get out of bed and walk us up and down the hospital corridor. He'd introduce us to the pretty nurses and show us Quebec sights from the windows.

Then, exhausted, he'd return to bed and ask for his pain medication. When he finally fell asleep, we'd leave and go sightseeing.

After a week the doctor took me aside and told me in French what the plan was (thank heavens for my French conversation refresher course—although it hadn't included vocabulary dealing with fatal illnesses). The plan was to send Boo back to the old folks' home the next day. Nurses there would take care of him until he died. Since the cancer had moved up towards the brain, first he'd slip into a coma, then he'd die.

It could take months.

Obviously, we weren't going to be able to stay until the end. The girls had to get back to school.

"Boo," I said to him later when we were alone. "Do you want to talk about your illness?" I'd read Kübler-Ross on death and dying and she'd said the patient should be encouraged to talk about it.

She didn't know Boo.

He shook his head: "Damn waste of time!"

Suddenly I felt stuck for things to say. Everything seemed to touch on areas that I was resentful about.

In fact, my resentment was getting in my way. I kept flashing on Inez's pronouncement: Someday you're going to have to handle your resentment towards your father head on.

"Someday" had arrived.

I sat there by the side of Boo's bed wondering how I was going to pull off telling a dying man he'd been a son-of-a-bitch all his life and I was angry about it.

Then it occurred to me why I was finding it so hard. My problem wasn't that he'd been a son-of-a-bitch; that was *his* problem. My problem was that I'd been angry about it and I'd never told him.

I told him now.

"Ever since I was a little kid I've been mad at you for things, Boo, and I never let you know how I felt, which wasn't fair. I was mad at you for leaving us. I was mad at you for not being a daddy to me. *Walt* had to do that—"

Boo made a face at the mention of Walt's name.

"—I was mad and hurt by that mean letter you wrote me after Mommy died—"

Boo looked confused when I mentioned the letter, but let me go on.

"—and most of all I was mad that you never sent us money. But I didn't tell you about it. I just didn't write. I kept it a secret. But every time you popped up that's what I thought about. I want you to know I'm more grown up than that now and I'm sorry."

The words poured out as though on tape and I could almost feel my anger begin to drain off. I wasn't sitting on it anymore. And in place of the anger was that strange warm feeling that had been awakened so many years before by my children—*love*.

When it was clear that I'd finished, Boo began to talk, although physically it was getting harder for him; the cancer had reached his throat. He paused between groups of words to get the strength to go on.

"Sylvia, I don't remember writing any letter after Bonnie died," he paused. "Maybe I was drunk. It hit me hard," he paused again. "I'm sorry if it upset you. Just ravings. *Not* intended. I'm sorry."

Then he laughed. Strange, I thought, after what I'd just said.

"So finally you get around to asking me..." another pause "...for money!"

"No, Boo, that's not what I meant!—"

He put up his hand to shut me up.

"I thought you'd never get around to it. You have such...stubborn pride, just like Bonnie. So boring!...Now you've made me (pause) happy. I feel needed." He grinned.

We were silent, holding hands.

"Sylvia, listen!" He leaned close to me. "Tomorrow you'll stop at the Banque de Quebec."

I was embarrassed. "Boo, really, that's not what I meant. I wasn't speaking about now. *Then* is what I was talking about."

"Please!" It was an order.


The next morning we found Boo standing by the nursing station in his wrinkled bathrobe, looking scrawny and unkempt, his toilet articles and other personal things in a paper sack. He looked like an inmate from one of those places he kept ending up in.

"Doesn't he have any clothes?" I asked a nurse.

"*Non*." Apparently that's what he'd arrived in. "But you go right away home, yes?" she said in English.

I looked at Boo. He had a devilish twinkle in his eye. Obviously he hadn't told them he was planning an errand. They'd have forbidden it for sure, which was probably just what Boo found so delicious.

It was a quiet morning in the wood-paneled, staid Banque de Quebec without much else to look at except Boo in his bathrobe, weak from being up on his feet for even this long, followed by me and then Emily and Abby—Emily oblivious, Abby self-conscious. I could almost hear the thoughts of the bank tellers—Who's the lunatic in the robe? And who's that woman with him? And does she have a gun in his side?

At a teller's window, Boo took a grungy wallet out of his paper sack. His checkbook and savings account passbook were in it. He opened the savings account book and showed it to the teller—then pointed to himself.

"You want the money from your account?" the teller asked in English.

Boo nodded.

"There's twelve hundred seventy-four dollars and forty-one cents. You want all of it?"

Boo nodded again.

"You want to close the account?"

Boo nodded. I shuddered.

"Canadian?"

Boo shook his head. "American," he said, nodding towards me.

"—less the exchange, of course," the teller said.

Boo nodded.

I stared down at my feet and tried to look innocent of any of this.

Next Boo opened his checkbook and went through the same procedure.

"There's six hundred three dollars and twelve cents. You want all of it?"

"No."

"How much?"

"Two hundred American." He nodded towards me. "Two hundred Canadian." He pointed towards himself.

"Bills," he said to me, as though explaining.

He'd left himself about four hundred dollars. How long would that last him, I found myself thinking—how *long*?

I felt a catch in my throat. This scene was going on forever!

The teller went to get the money.

"You don't have to do this!" I said.

"*Have* to. If I don't (pause)...some petty bourgeois government official will come in (pause) the minute I die (he'd said the word!)...and *take* it!" He grinned. "You're going to smuggle it out of Canada for me—and keep it as your reward."

He seemed delighted with the whole thing.

I couldn't help but smile.

Boo, clasping the money in his fist, led the way as we walked painfully slowly out of the bank. Once outside, he grabbed both my hands and joyfully slapped the money into my palms. Emily was wandering down the street. Abby was watching, fascinated. I could read her mind: new clothes!

The next day we left for California.

One last time Boo refused his morning pain medication to stay clear-headed. One last time he insisted on our walk—this time through the lobby, down the front stairs of the home and across the parking lot to our car. He was carrying his old beat-up briefcase with the buckles; I remembered it from when I was a kid. It contained the manuscript of a one-thousand-page novel he'd never sold. At the car he handed it over to me.

"I don't want the Canadians to have it," he said.

We said our last goodbyes. "Seatbelts on, girls"..."write" ..."send copies of the pictures you took"..."get well soon"...

Driving out of the parking lot I could see him in the rearview mirror as he waved and smiled weakly—and then I saw a nurse come quickly to his side and grab his arm—no need to play strong anymore. I saw him almost collapse gratefully onto the support of her arm as she began to lead him back across the parking lot towards the Home.

"Mom, I have watery eyes," Emily said as we pulled out of the drive and onto the street. "Can you see I have watery eyes?" It was Emily's way of telling us she felt sad.

"Yes. I feel sad, too."

Abby was openly crying. "It's not fair! We just met him and he's dying. You said he was so terrible. He gave us all that money. You should have brought us up here before."

There was anger in her at me—for that, and probably for a lot of other things she wasn't even conscious of—for my sins.

"I probably should have," I said.

In Las Vegas, on our last night on the road, I had a blow-up with Emily after she got lost walking to an ice cream place.

She was scared and I was panicky. "Why didn't you go back to our hotel?"

"I didn't know which one it was."

"You don't even know the *name*?"

"You didn't tell me."

I exploded. "Emily, what am I going to do with you!? Stop being so helpless! The name of the hotel is written everywhere. I *assumed* you'd noticed. You've got to start noticing things going on around you! You're not a little girl anymore! You've got to learn to fend for yourself! You've got to be independent—"

"Mom!—"

"What!"

"You *know* when you yell I make myself deaf."

I went down an octave. "Emily, I worry about you. What would you do if you were with me someplace and I dropped dead? Tell me! What would you do? How would you save yourself?"

She thought a moment and then in all sincerity said, "Call Daddy?"

I laughed. I had to. Either that or cry.

When we got back to Los Angeles there was a message on my answering machine from Boo's old folks' home. He'd slipped into a coma only two days after we'd left. It was just a matter of time.

I'd keep waking up in the middle of the night picturing myself dead and Emily a bag lady, helpless, defenseless, impoverished—with neither Sandy nor I still around to take care of her.

"She needs a training program for independent living," a social worker friend casually mentioned.

"What's that?"

"It's to teach her how to fend for herself and not be dependent on you and Sandy."

That was the answer!

I took Emily for yet another evaluation. Over the years she'd had a string of them and a string of nearly useless diagnoses and useless referrals to go with them, starting with that "in the direction of autism" diagnosis at the age of two-and-a-half and going from there to neurotic, to schizophrenic, to brain-damaged, to mildly retarded to "willful and spoiled." When it came to school, she was put in special education classes with a diagnosis of "learning disabilities." Now I had a new referral to a doctor at a university medical center who'd spent thirty years of his life researching autism. Why hadn't I been told about him before? These things made me furious. Help was like a secret you had to ferret out.

The kindly doctor saw her three times and Sandy and me twice. I filled out a long questionnaire and got to ask him lots of questions—like could Doriden have hurt Emily. (So far no one knows.)

"She's a high-functioning autistic" was his conclusion. "We're just beginning to recognize this as a diagnosis. Autism runs on a continuum, just like alcoholism does. (He knew about me.) It goes from the very mild to the very severe. Not all autistics are plate-spinners, just like not all alcoholics are skid row bums. Kids like Emily who are high-functioning fall between the cracks all the time."

"Tell me about it!" I said.

Ironically, Emily had given herself a similar diagnosis years before. (But who ever listens to "crazies"?) We'd been watching a TV show together about a severely autistic little boy. Afterwards Emily said to me: "The difference between that little boy and me is that he's *stuck* in his dreamworld, but I can make myself come out of mine whenever I want to. And *I* don't spin plates!"

I'd given her a hug. Now the trick was to help her want to come out of her dreamworld and stay out long enough to learn how to survive in the real world!

On the basis of this doctor's report Emily was accepted by Regional Center for state funding. When she got out of high school, her independent living training would be arranged and paid for. What a relief!

Five weeks after Boo had gone into the coma he died. I took the next day off from work, had the girls excused from school, and we went to the beach for a picnic and some remembering.

"Remember the horse and buggy ride we took in Quebec, Mom?" said Abby. "Remember the time Boo gave us all that money and we ate outside at that expensive restaurant? Wasn't that nice, Emily?"

We both turned to look at Emily and get her response.

Emily had watery eyes.

# – 28 –

# A CAVE IN MANHATTAN

*We have what we seek. It is there all the time, and if we give it time it will make itself known to us.*
— *Thomas Merton*

Some people have to go all the way to India and sit in a cave to discover that The Answers are within.

I had to go to New York.

People may try to save you the trouble by *telling* you the answers are within, but it's not the same. You have to find out for yourself.

Once I decided my answers lay in Manhattan, there was no stopping me—although I had a couple of friends who tried.

"You're doing a geographic," one said, meaning I was running away. "You don't have to go anywhere to find yourself." Interestingly enough, her thing was being afraid to drive freeways. "The answers are all in your own backyard."

"For you they'd better be or you're out of luck," I said back, rubbing it in.

Of course the big fear underlying all this resistance I was running into was that I'd push too far into the red zone, that danger area, and drink again. For an alcoholic, making a cross-country move was definitely seen as red zone material.

"Nothing is going to be different in New York. Every place is the same as every other place," said another friend.

"Oh, come on, Cheryl! You're telling me Tierra del Fuego is the same as Detroit? I'm talking about *consciousness*, not buildings! Like in New York men don't gag when they have to talk to a woman over thirty the way they do here."

"Men are equally disappointing everywhere." She was a bit disappointed herself.

"At least in New York they'll be wearing suits. I just can't wait to sashay through the bar at P.J. Clarke's and look at a few of them."

"The *bar*?"

I really was making people nervous. "It's a restaurant too."

I'd started getting my "visions" again, just the way I did before making the trip to Quebec to see Boo. Driving along a freeway, suddenly I'd "see" a street in Greenwich Village or Connecticut and I'd have such a longing to be there I could hardly bear it.

But there was a lot to handle first before I could think about leaving Los Angeles for New York—like who'd go with me.

"You brought me here to California; you take me home," I said to Sandy. I wasn't resurrecting the idea of marriage. I just thought it would be nice to have someone I cared about living in the same town.

He shook his head. "Uh-uh. When I retire I'm going the other way."

"Hell?"

"Hawaii."

"How can you retire to a place that doesn't have a subway?"

Funny, here Sandy was talking about retirement and I still didn't even know what I wanted to be when I grew up!

Next I approached Abby about the idea of moving to New York.

"I don't want to live in New York," she said. "I hate all that weather. It's too dark."

"It's not *dark*. You've just seen too many black and white photographs."

"No, it's dark. And I'll miss my friends. My roots are here."

"You can make *new* roots."

"Mom, you don't understand. The only thing I remember about New York is there's a *dog* there."

"If we find that same dog, will you go?"

"No way, Jose. I'm moving in with Daddy."

Emily would have gone with me in a minute, but I said no. It was too important for her to get the two years of independent living training that she'd been funded for—although frankly she wasn't crazy about the idea of independent living.

"Mom, do I have to learn responsibilities? When I get out of high school can't I just stay with you?"

190

Sometimes that sounded so appealing. Then I could keep my eye on her, make sure she was safe and didn't wander away or get ripped-off (in school she was always getting ripped-off) or raped or kidnapped or murdered. Then I wouldn't have to deal with all those agencies, all those interviews. Emily was content to stay alone for days at a time—listening to her music, or walking around the dining-room table smiling about her fantasies, or watching TV. She loved TV. She was so little trouble really—

But then I'd wake up again in the middle of the night and think about what would happen to her if Sandy and I died. A bag lady fate—or worse? Just the thought of it would put a stop to my fantasy that living with me was Emily's solution.

She absolutely had to get free of me.

The next interview for Emily was with the "Feds" to see if she was eligible for government disability. That was crucial. She would have money for rent and food once she moved into her independent living apartment. Without it, she couldn't go.

All the way to the Federal building in Westwood for the interview I was itching to tell her, "When you go in there, Emily, *act disabled!*" but I refrained. I just knew she'd blow the whistle on me, "Am I acting disabled okay, Mom?"

As it turned out, Emily didn't need instructions. She did beautifully on her own. She chattered on and on in her sweet, dingbatty way, asking the young male interviewer highly inappropriate personal questions ("Are you still a virgin?") and whenever she wasn't talking, she pulled little hairs out of the back of her hand by their roots.

She was accepted for SSI disability benefits.

"Congratulations!" I said. "Your learning disabilities are paying off! I'm proud of you."

Emily liked that.

It looked like my New York adventure was on.

I took my first steps into the red zone by giving up my little house in Brentwood and putting everything in storage, except for what I'd need for those few months it was going to take me (or so I thought) to get my act together in the Big Apple. Emily and Abby and the cat moved in with Sandy, and I moved in temporarily with my godmother, Mattie, a writer and all-round dynamic lady in her seventies.

A few days after I moved in—after all the distractions of packing and unpacking were over and I had time to think—I went into a tailspin.

I woke up one morning with a full-scale anxiety attack, the worst I'd had in years, and it went on for days.

I was mystified. *Why?*

"Sylvie, calm down! Listen to me! Read my lips!" my sister Justine said to me on the phone from New York. "You just gave up your house. You just gave up your kids. You just gave up all your furniture and all your things. You're about to give up your job and your car and move three thousand miles away to a city you haven't lived in for years where you've got no job waiting, no money to speak of—and no relationship to help make all the rest a little easier. You've gone and created the empty nest syndrome for yourself years ahead of schedule and you've even chucked the nest! And you wonder why you feel anxious! Sylvie, sometimes you amaze me. You're the psychotherapist. Do you think that means you're *above* feelings?"

As Abby would have said, "Busted!"

I was eleven years sober and feeling shaky as a newcomer with flare-ups of those geekpit feelings. Max, my new (and first male) mentor and his wife let me tag along after them to some parties so I wouldn't have to be alone.

After a week I began to feel whole again.

I'd survived those first few steps into the red zone without falling back into a bottle of gin.

Soon I'd be ready to step out even further.

Emily graduated from high school. The "special ed" students wore the same white caps and gowns as the rest of the class. Emily looked breathtakingly beautiful—but she was worried.

"Mom, when I march out there, do you think people can tell I have learning disabilities?"

"No." Then I said, pretending to be worried too, "Do you think people can tell I have alcoholism?"

"No," she said, seriously.

"Well, do you think they can tell Abby sees auras?"

"No," she said again.

"What about Daddy? Do you think people can tell he's a loner?"

"No!" Now she was smiling?

"—In fact, *President* of the Loners Clubs of America?"

"No!"

"Well, *I* think we all hide our weirdness very well, don't you?"

192

That made her laugh. "Yes!"

She glowed all day.

"You know, Mattie," I said to my godmother, "I'm an official orphan now. Mother is dead. Daddy is dead. Boo is dead. That means it's up to you to raise me, wasn't that the deal?"

"I'll do my very best."

I think she meant it. Every night she'd sit up and wait for me to get home from my job as an alcoholism therapist or from a recovery group meeting or a date.

"Tell me, Sylvie dear, what goes? Come and sit and we'll have a chat. Now, tell me all about your patients? Was this the night you had your women's group at the hospital or was this the night you had a date with that architect?"

Mattie was a glutton for information. The writer in her never slept. She was always picking brains during her chats. She read a couple of books a week, but that wasn't enough. She much preferred to hear about things right from the horse's mouth. No matter who came into her sphere, she'd light up: "Come, sit, we'll have a chat. Tell me, what goes?"

Without knowing it, Mattie helped me with my problem of being too judgmental. One day I asked her: "What's the secret of having so many friends?" She had them in all age groups, from four years old on up.

"We all have to learn to put up with each other," she said simply.

For some reason, I'd never thought of that before!

Abby began her last year of high school. Popular and beautiful, she was doing a lot of socializing and a lot of cheerleading but very little aura reading.

"I don't want anyone to know I do that, Mom! Don't you even know how freaky that is?"

"I just hate to see you let a talent like that atrophy, Abby. You really should keep it up."

"Oh, Mom!"

I went to the Bodhi Tree and bought her three books on aura reading.

She stuck the books under her bed.

Emily began her independent living program in Santa Monica called Project Lift. She moved into one of their special apartments, had a roommate (another Project Lift client) and was already learning some of the skills she'd need to survive without me: cooking, cleaning, shopping, money management, personal hygiene, safety, socialization skills, transportation, assertion training. The works.

But on her first night in her new apartment I couldn't stand leaving my little baby all alone without her mama so I slept on the floor in the living room. On the second night I weaned myself away after dinner and on the third night I phoned.

In early October I left for New York.

The drive-away agency car I was to deliver turned out to be a new baby blue Cadillac Coupe de Ville. I loaded it to the gills. I said my goodbyes to Mattie and drove straight to the Marina for my farewell brunch with Sandy and the girls.

Abby openly wept into her omelette.

"I'm going to miss you so much I can't stand it!"

She was breaking my heart.

"Why do you have to do this?" she went on. "Why can't you just stay put and be happy?"

She was beginning to sound like Sandy.

"Because I'm 'into' things, remember?"

Emily was easier: she just sat there at the table quietly stuffing her face (she was into overeating) and picking the hairs out of the backs of her hands. I'd finally figured out that she did both these things when she was nervous. "How much longer are we going to be here, Mom?"

"Why?"

"I don't want to miss my T.V. shows."

As I drove out of Los Angeles towards Barstow, a fake male protector/companion under a cowboy hat with a towel for a head by my side, I asked myself a similar question, "What the hell *am* I doing this for? Being a gypsy when you're in your twenties is one thing, but uprooting your whole life in your forties when you don't even have to is crazy!"

Yet the idea of not doing it was worse.

I went south through the Texas Panhandle to avoid any early fall snow. It was hot. The country music on the radio was all about raw passions. I sensed a hovering sensuality out there on the plain. I felt lonely, homesick, afraid. I got telephonitis. Every night from the motel I called one coast or the other just to reassure myself that I hadn't disappeared.

194

I arrived in Manhattan a week later on a mild mid-October day. The leaves in Central Park were brilliantly colored. People were sunning themselves on the steps of the Metropolitan Museum of Art. The outdoor restaurants and cafes made the city look like Paris. It was fast-paced, stimulating and exciting—but the one feeling that I'd been anticipating and hoping for, the feeling of "I'm home," just didn't happen. I was disappointed. I wanted it to be there because that's the feeling commitment springs from. I needed to be committed to this move. But it simply wasn't there.

That was not a good omen.

I unpacked my worldly goods and stuffed them into every nook and cranny of the maid's room in my Aunt Ramona's Lexington Avenue apartment which was to be my home until I "made it" in the big city.

The room was tiny; it was like living in the camper again, but I knew enough to be grateful for it. The location was terrific. There were bars on the window, a fire escape outside, and cockroach races up and down the wall at night.

My first Manhattan purchase was a Roach Motel.

When my sister's little daughter referred to my maid's room as "Auntie Sylvie's cave," I figured I'd died and gone to India after all.

"How the hell did I end up here?" I sniveled to my mentor Max in a long distance phone call.

"You haven't 'ended up' yet," he said. "Your story isn't over, at least not until the fat lady sings. In the meantime, get yourself to some recovery group meetings. You'll feel better. And just remember, I love you—and if you drink again I'll stab you."

I assumed I'd find a job working as a psychotherapist in the chemical dependency field. But after a month of interviews I reached an unanticipated conclusion: I didn't want to do that any more—at least not here in New York. I wasn't sure why—but I just couldn't get revved up about it. I didn't care.

What, I thought, do I do now?

My answer came in one word—*computers*—said to me by Justine in passing, "Remember Beth? She's writing for a computer magazine. You should talk to her."

I knew right then and there that my mission in Manhattan would be to learn about computers.

I could just hear Abby now:

"Oh, yes, my Mom's living in New York and she's 'into' computers."

There was just one minor hitch.

I had never even touched one.

A whirlwind self-education spree would fix that.

I began by using my first rule of thumb: "Start anywhere."

I signed up for a one-hour, $75.00 class in microcomputers at a computer store just off Wall Street—too much money for too little time, I later concluded, but it served its purpose, it got me going.

Besides, I was enlightened there.

"You wanna know what the difference between hardware and software is?" the instructor asked. "If you drop hardware on your foot, it hurts. If you drop software on your foot, it doesn't."

Fantastic!

In another class in another store, the instructor said: "Don't be afraid to touch the computer keyboard. Pushing the wrong key won't blow up the machine."

That's *just* what I'd been worrying about—that I'd blow up the machine or that if I pushed the wrong key, somebody would die.

I read, read, read, especially computer magazines, especially the ads. Ads taught me a lot.

I watched TV shows about computers. I read the Tuesday computer section in the *New York Times*, front to back.

I eavesdropped on computer conversations in buses and subways and coffee shops, and I signed up for a string of adult education classes.

I got as far as a job interview at one store but was told I needed "hands-on" experience first.

Frustrating. I was dying for hands-on experience. I just didn't have a computer to put my hands on.

One Tuesday I saw a notice in the *Times* for an all-afternoon seminar on word-processing programs for writers. It was to be held at a computer store in Greenwich Village near New York University.

I was there.

It was a funky place; they looked like they'd been in business twenty minutes. They catered to academics instead of business folk. Immediately I felt at home. It dawned on me that my niche in the computer world might involve talking to writers about how to use computers for their work. Meanwhile I could learn about using computers for *my* work.

It was perfect.

196

After the seminar I went up to the owner.

"I have a proposition. I'll work here for a month for *free*. I'll do anything you need done—I'll answer phones, sweep floors, paint, decorate the window, file, run errands—if, in between, you'll let me get some practice on your machines. At the end of the month if you think I've learned enough to sell, I'd like you to take me on as a saleswoman. Deal?"

The owner thought about it.

"Deal."

Now it was official: Mom-in-Motion was "into" computers in New York!

With the job thing settled, at least for now, I turned my attention to other parts of my New York life.

It wasn't looking good.

My main problem was that I still hadn't felt that "I'm home" feeling— and I'd been there three months. It was like I was "doing time."

I went to some recovery meetings and began to meet people, but I kept having judgmentalness attacks: meetings are better in L.A.; they don't know how to do it right here; these people don't even know how to use a microphone so the audience can hear them talk...

"You're pretty fussy about the recovery group that saved your life!" Mentor Max reminded me on the telephone. "So what I want you to do is go to those meetings until you start liking them again."

"You mean I'm being 'resistant'?"

"If you want to put it in shrink terms, yes."

Those psychotherapy words could still get a rise out of me!

"Okay," I said reluctantly.

One of the things I liked best about New York was the walking. I walked everywhere. I walked between three and five miles a day—to work, home from work, to meetings, home from meetings.

But when the cold weather really hit, my walks were curbed and I took it hard.

"I hate this weather," I bitched to Max. "It feels like the skin on my face is getting attacked by little pinchy lobster claws. I hate it, hate it."

"What we resist persists," he teased.

"Oh, don't tell me that! At the rate I'm fighting it, it'll never be spring!"

The cold weather showed up the city's mean side. I was unsettled by the rich/poor contrasts. It was like Versailles before the French Revolution—and I wasn't sure I wanted to stay around for the war. And I was upset by the plight of the homeless. They were everywhere—on the sidewalk in front of elegant store windows, outside the gold-leaf Helmsley Palace, on the steps of Grand Central Station (which reeked of urine), on the subway gratings, on the steps of churches.

It was the bag ladies that bothered me the most. I couldn't help but see Emily—"there but for the grace of God," etc. One night I saw a toothless woman, obviously schizophrenic, who was nearly shaking apart from the bitter cold. She was wearing only a short skirt, no stockings and a thin sweater. Next to her on the steps was a brightly wrapped Christmas present.

When I got back to my tiny but warm room, I couldn't sleep. Things about the world were *hurting* me!

The Sufis, a religious sect, say that we have to resign ourselves to the fact that the world is both incredibly tender and incredibly brutal.

I was happy to be awake and sober for all the tender stuff. It was the brutal stuff I was having trouble with. In fact, at times like this I was even able to say to myself: "Now I know why I drank!"

I met some men.

But underneath the suits and manners (which I still liked) they were about the same. One I dated definitely needed assertiveness training. On the fourth date as we were coming out of a movie (it was only 9:50) he said, "Do you think you ought to be getting home?—or what?" It wasn't a very seductive line. I took a bus home.

Then I met a man at a party that New Yorkers would probably have described as "interesting" (they do love that word!) and Californians would have called a "head-tripper." After spending three-and-a-half hours talking to me and nobody else but me (I was *sure* he'd ask me out) he said, "You're a very interesting woman, Sylvia. You have a mind like a finely tuned Porsche. You'd be perfect for me. Unfortunately, what I want is to marry and have kids of my own."

It wasn't so much his conclusion that I objected to as the fact that it took him so long to arrive at it. If he had told me this at the beginning of our conversation, I might have been young enough to fit into his plans.

And then there was one of the Disappeared Ones who over a period of weeks wooed me, dined me, bedded me—and then disappeared.

No phone call. Nothing. The next time I ran into him I went right up to his face: "Tell me, did you think if you disappeared I wouldn't notice?"

I was sick and tired of such acts going unmentioned!

The owner of the computer store was true to his word. I'd learned a lot and he took me on as a saleswoman for $200 a week—plus commissions.

It was another two months before I made my first sale!

Abby was turned down at UCLA. She was crushed. She made tearful phone calls to me. She felt her life was ruined. It just killed me to be so far away from her when she was having a broken heart.

She pulled through admirably; I was proud of her for being resilient and told her so. But it wasn't the same as being there to hug her.

One day I was walking along lower Fifth Avenue past a quaint old church; it reminded me of a street in Paris. Then a thought went through my head: "Hmmmmm, Sylvia, maybe The Answers aren't in New York City after all. Maybe what you should have done was move to Paris…"

That's when I knew that my wandering had to stop.

# – 29 –

# A GROWN-UP MAN

*For two personalities to meet is like mixing two chemical substances; if there is any combination at all, both are transformed.*

—Carl Jung

*You are doomed to be happy in wedlock.*
—*Fortune cookie message saved from 1978*

One more time I set off across America in a drive-away agency car with my fake male protector/companion, now named "John Wayne," by my side under a cowboy hat. "John" made me feel safer on lonely stretches when I had those killer thoughts about being done in by highway banditos.

I dipped further south this trip so I could visit a friend in Houston. She'd left Los Angeles two years earlier to seek The Answers in a Texas ad agency—that was *her* cave.

"The Houston vibes are mystical and eerie," I said after my first day. "I can see why you like it here. Maybe it's the heat. It feels like angel wings are hovering over the place."

Then I added, "How are the men?"

We went to a country dance hall just to stare at men two-stepping around a dance floor. It was P.J. Clarke's all over again, except these men had on tight jeans and boots instead of three-piece suits and penny loafers.

"At least they don't look wimpy dressed like that."

Halfway across the desolate 750-mile stretch of Texas Interstate 10 between Houston and the New Mexico border, I celebrated my twelfth year of sobriety. Twelve years without gin or Valium or grass or Dexedrine or LSD or any of it. And ten without a cigarette. I'd been sober longer than I drank. But whenever I saw a billboard showing a martini glass with those beads of water dripping down the side my mouth still watered; I could taste it. I could smell it. But the obsession center in my body that would have made me drink was still asleep. If that should ever wake up again *that's* when I'd be in trouble.

I called Max from a phone booth in Senora so he could congratulate me.

"Congratulations, kid."

"Thanks, Max. Christ, it's lonely out here! It's so good to hear your voice. Now I don't feel so far from home."

I'd said the word—home.

Now I was going home to California.

The first time I'd been brought to L.A., now I was choosing it.

I hung up the phone and walked back to my car. On the way I picked up a little tumbleweed and stuck it in the back seat. I'd keep it as a symbol of my wanderlust.

When I arrived at last in "Shaky City" (as the truckers call L.A. on their CB's) and the desert dry heat of a May "Santa Ana" hit me, I felt excited. "Damn, Sylvia!" I said to myself. "Whatever made you think you could be happy in New York in the wintertime when you know how much you love heat?"

I crashed at my friend Harriet's, paid visits to Emily and Abby (who were happy that Mom-in-Motion had finally come home) and within twenty-four hours I lined up a job as a therapist in a chemical dependency hospital, sublet a house with a pool (already things were looking better than that maid's room in Manhattan), and managed to borrow a car.

I had about everything I wanted except, of course—Him.

When I got moved and settled I sent for a booklet on some community adult education classes. I signed up for an eight week computer class. I'd worked hard to learn what little I knew about computers; I didn't want to lose touch altogether.

The class I chose was in BASIC, the most commonly used computer programming language. Not that I planned to do any programming, I didn't. But being the kind of character who has to take clocks apart to see how they tick, I wanted to know what was behind the word-processing programs I was now using for my writing. What made them tick?

I showed up for the first class and did my usual quick scan of the room to check it out for husband material. I did this everywhere I went, even funerals. My conclusion was No, so I settled down to learn some BASIC.

At the end of the sixth class the instructor told us that he was going on a two-week vacation. He wrote the name of the substitute teacher on the board and like a good little student I copied it down in my notebook: Lance.

Lance turned out to be marvelous looking—tall and lean (not too lean) with deep blue eyes, full mouth, uneven nose, a lot of hair, great voice and a rather cornball sense of humor. I thought I detected the faintest trace of an accent—instead of "zero" he said "siro."

He was a good teacher. I began understanding things that had been baffling me.

In class he talked about his son. He must be married. Too bad.

After the last class I went up to thank him. I told him I'd just moved back from New York. He told me he was Danish (which explained the accent). I told him I was about to drive my daughter to Colorado for her first year of college. He told me he wrote software (now I knew what software was). He gave me his card. I gave him my card.

And that was it.

I left and thought no more about him.

When I got back from Colorado I signed up for another computer class, part two of BASIC. I noticed that Lance was the teacher; I was glad. I remembered he was good.

I stopped by his desk to say hello.

"How was New York?" he said. I hadn't even had a chance to remind him we'd met before. Hmmm.

"It was Colorado. I was in New York, but that was before."

"Colorado, of course! I knew the minute 'New York' was out of my mouth it was wrong. Serves me right for trying to be Mr. Cool."

That wasn't like a married man, to be embarrassed about getting some detail of my life mixed up. Hmmmmmm.

That's when he asked me out for coffee.

Maybe he wasn't married!

Suddenly I wanted to kick myself for being dressed in a sweatsuit.

"My son lives with me, he's eleven. My other son is four. He lives with my ex-wife," Lance told me.

So, here I am again, I thought, sitting in yet another coffee shop behind another cup of coffee across from another Mr. Potential. In twelve years I must have had a thousand cups of coffee while in the process of sizing up a man. By now I was good at it. I could usually tell if it was a No even before the coffee arrived. A Yes was always trickier. There were even different kinds of Yes.

"My wife left me to go out and 'find' herself," Lance was saying. "I was buried in my computer. I didn't see it coming. It taught me a lesson: People come before programs."

Just the thought of having to go out and find oneself filled me with exhaustion—better her than me!

"I'm glad I don't have to do *that* one again," I said.

That's when it hit me that the reason I didn't have to go out and do that one again was because I'd already done it! Somewhere along the line I'd *found* myself! Son-of-a-gun! When did it happen? What day?

"I just realized something," I said. "I know who I am!" I said that as much to myself as to Lance. It was an awakening. It gave me goosebumps.

"I'm glad to hear that!" Lance answered and gave a little laugh.

We talked, and as we talked a part of my brain stood back and did its automatic, somewhat jaded evaluation of the scene. It went like this:

This conversation is going both ways; the talk is synergistic. (That's a good omen.) I'm not having to think of things to say. (Whew!) He's paying absolute attention to me. (Very exciting!) He's asking good questions about me and about my work. (He's not egocentric.) He's also sharing. (He's not withholding.) He's giving me immediate feed-back, like "Oh, interesting you should say that..." (Good sign. I know where he stands moment to moment.) He's opinionated in places, even judgmental. (But look who's talking!) He smokes. (I could do without that! Just like Sandy!)

I kept trying to remind myself, "Sylvia, he didn't ask you to marry him, he just asked you out for coffee!"

It didn't help. I kept right on evaluating.

I dragged out my dusty "Must" list and reviewed it in my mind. Chemistry? Yes, that's here. (Thank God! Without that, all the rest of this stuff is irrelevant.) Integrity? I think so; he keeps referring to his responsibilities—to his kids, to his work and, strangely, to The Truth. Conductor Zubin Mehta's wife once said that the sexiest thing about Zubin was his integrity. Maybe that was Lance, too.

"It's fun just sitting here talking like this," Lance said. (How cute! He actually thought we were just sitting there talking!) "I'm enjoying myself."

I was astounded that a man would come right out and say a thing like that to a woman. Didn't he know enough to be wary and on guard? Wasn't he hip enough to be afraid of being vulnerable? Wasn't he cool enough to be nervous that I'd take his spontaneous comment as some kind of commitment? Where'd he *been*, for chrissake?

"I'm enjoying it too," I said back.

"Tell me about alcoholism. I know nothing about it. If I have two beers a year I feel very wild."

So he was a "normie." In my recovery group that's what we call people who don't have a drinking problem. I was relieved Lance was a "normie." Even more than most people, recovering alcoholics are afraid of falling in love with drinkers. The reason is obvious—drinkers can so easily pull us back down into the geek pit where we came from. And most of us don't *ever* want to be there again.

"How did you get into the alcoholism field?" he asked.    Oh-oh, Sylvia! I said to myself. Here's where you get your big chance to tell him—too soon—that you not only *work* with alcoholics, you *are* one. I'd played this shock game before: "Love me, love my disease!"

But a little voice inside of me (I think she was getting tired of being single, too!) said: "Shut up, Sylvia, for once in your life shut up! You don't have to Show and Tell all your liabilities the first night. Deep six The Truth and save the stretchmarks for later. Capisce?"

Got it.

"One summer I volunteered at the National Council on Alcoholism," I said, "and that's how I got interested in the field of chemical dependency." (That sounded a little better than "alcoholism.")

"Ah-hah, I see," Lance said.

That answer would do for now.

After coffee he drove me back to my car and we sat in the parking

205

lot in front of the school and talked some more. Politics. More than once I pictured kissing his face.

"Can you debate a political issue without getting mad?" he suddenly asked.

I nodded. "I can also get mad without debating a political issue."

I thought that was kind of clever, but Lance went right on. He was getting increasingly energized. "If you can debate without getting mad, let's debate something." He made himself more comfortable in his seat. "This is fun!"

They say you shouldn't pray for things or you might get them. I used to pray for somebody who was the opposite of Silent Sandy—somebody who was a real talker.

God gave me Lance!

Two hours later we called a halt to our third or fourth debate and said good night. I drove home, exhausted but happy. I'd had a marvelous time.

Strangely, in spite of all that, I thought about Lance very little during the week. That in itself was proof he wasn't one of the Obsessives I was so inclined to fall for—someone I'd end up taking hostage after a few dates and then cling to like a two-toed sloth for fear that if I stopped obsessing about him for even an instant he'd disappear.

It wasn't like that with Lance. When I did think about him it felt good, but if I never saw him again that would be okay, too.

But there had been a kind of perfection to the evening; it felt complete. Lance had given me a gift. He'd shown me there were still nice men out there who could be attracted to me and vice-versa.

If *he* was out there, then others were out there.

It gave me hope.

I maintained my cool and felt just fine when I walked into the next computer class.

Also I made sure I dressed better.

But seeing Lance in the flesh again stirred up my classic alcoholic greediness: I wanted more. I wanted more of going out for coffee, I wanted more of talking, I wanted more of debating, I wanted more of looking at him, I wanted more of good feelings, and I wanted more of things I hadn't even had any of yet. I wanted the bottle of All-Heal and tonight the All-Heal was Lance. No wonder recovering alcoholics kiddingly call alcoholism "More's Disease!" There's the joke about the alcoholic who goes into a bar and sees a sign: "All you can drink for $1.00." The alcoholic says to the bartender, "Give me two dollars' worth."

That's alcoholism. And that's me!

I debated: Should I ask him out for coffee? Or shouldn't I ask him? Will he ask me? Or won't he ask me?

It started to make me crazy.

Had the class ended sooner, I'd probably have asked him out just to break the tension. It would have been like a "fix."

But fifteen minutes before the witching hour I had another "flash experience," similar to the ones I'd had about both cigarettes and gin, except this one was about men:

"No More Chasing Men!"

That was what Pauline and Inez and Max had been telling me for years. But being a feminist it had always struck me as archaic advice— even downright suicidal for women over forty. "I could die waiting," I'd said.

But on this night something inside of me snapped and the huntress in me went on strike. No more hunting. No more doing 80 percent of the work in a relationship so it wouldn't crumble. No more trying to fan a man's ambivalence into love. No more worrying, "Does he really want to be here?"

If the price I had to pay for this decision was being alone, I'd gladly pay it. I had my answer: If this man wants me, he's going to have to come and *get* me!

With that, I relaxed. Whew! It was amazing. Now there was nothing left for me to do. I no longer had to make something "happen." It was out of my hands. It was up to Lance, God, and the Universe—but it wasn't up to me.

When class was over I picked up my books, smiled goodbye to Lance and walked out of the room. Actually, I ran out of the room to make up for an equal and opposite desire within me to linger.

I was at the bottom of the outside stairs, about to push through the double glass doors to the street, when I heard him.

"Hey!" He was on the landing, looking breathless. He pantomimed drinking a cup of coffee and then he waited for my response.

My heart did a flip. I nodded yes.

He smiled. "I'll meet you outside. I've got to go back and get my stuff."

"I had to cut three students short just to follow you before you disappeared," Lance told me in the coffee shop. "You move fast! But something inside of me said, 'Quick! Follow that woman!' I don't usually do that."

"I'm glad you did." Later on I'd tell him the rest of it.

He asked me back to his apartment to see his computers. "Sorry, no etchings."

There was that slightly corny humor again.

We sat cross-legged on the floor next to each other in front of one of his computers while he showed me games he'd written. I drank him in. (What beautiful blue pool eyes you have; what marvelous hands.) I wanted to phone Justine in New York: "Jus, he's got Daddy's hands, isn't that great!" Twice our knees touched accidentally and I felt some of that good old-fashioned electricity. What a treat it was to feel all that. How nice it was to be sober.

I was glad Lance didn't make a move at me; it would have spoiled the fun of the preliminaries.

"Are you free Sunday night?" he asked as we walked out to my car. "I'd like to have a regular date."

"Yes."

"Max, I think I've found him. I don't want to do anything to mess it up! But what about my secrets? I have to tell him I'm an alcoholic. I have to tell him I'm older than he is (about five years was what I'd calculated). I have to tell him about Emily. I have to tell him I'm broke. What if these things bother him?"

"'The men who matter don't mind; the men who mind don't matter,'" Max said.

Sunday was another scorcher. I wore a white peasanty skirt, a loose-fitting pale pink blouse and white drippy flowers in my hair. Tan and a regular at Jane Fonda's Workout, I was in pretty good shape.

We'd arranged to meet at six at Lance's apartment after he'd dropped off his kids at his ex-wife's—a plan that was a set-up for a screw-up if I'd been dealing with an even mildly ambivalent man. ("Gosh, I *tried* calling you to tell you I'd be late, but you'd left...") But Lance was on the button.

"You'll find I'm obsessed with punctuality. If I'm even a minute late it makes me feel awful all day."

I liked it that he said, "You'll find..." It hinted at longevity.

At an Italian restaurant, we had a long, talkative dinner and then went back to his apartment for a little jazz (he'd been a jazz musician for years and before that a soccer player) followed by a delightful seduction.

Even in bed he talked and kept telling me, "This is fun!"

The next day, of course, I braced myself for the inevitable—no phone call.

Lance called me at work. "Hello there."

"Who is this?" I snapped.

"Lance. You do remember me?"

"God, I'm sorry! I mean I'm surprised you're actually calling me the next day."

"I wanted to tell you what a great time I had last night."

"Do you have any idea how rare you are?"

"I knew I was wonderful, but I didn't know I was rare."

"Rare. Believe me!"

"What's the deal with this guy, Max?" I said on the phone. "When is the other shoe going to drop? When am I going to discover he lets the air out of people's tires after midnight?"

"Maybe what he is is a grown-up—like the one you threw away when you left home. You've been given a second shot at it—so *enjoy* it!"

"I am! I am!"

Towards the end of the week Lance called me at home after work. "How'd you like to have dinner?"

"I'd love it. I'll meet you at your apartment." Lance lived forty minutes away. It was automatic for me to offer to go out of my way for a man's convenience.

"Don't you want me to pick you up?"

"I don't want you to have to drive all that way. I don't mind."

"Don't you think you're worth it?"

I could feel myself blush on the phone—busted again!

"Pick me up!" I said.

A week later he asked me over to dinner to meet his sons. I sat at the dining-room table with Alan, the eleven-year-old, and must have looked at a thousand baseball cards while trying to get a bead on him. There was something familiar about Alan—then I knew what it was.

209

He was *me* at eleven—a little defensive and insecure. Steven, four, was a clone of Lance. When we had dessert and lit candles and turned off all the lights, Steven was intrigued. "This is *fun!*" he said.

The next week Lance asked me to come over and bring my computer with me so we could be together but still do our separate work. Another elephant chip for me in New York had been recognizing how important it was for me to write. The whole computer thing had been about writing, not computers. When I was writing it was the only time I didn't feel I should be doing something else.

"It's so *nice* having you here," he said. "It feels so cozy. I love it that you're a writer, that you have something creative of your own to do. That way I don't feel guilty sitting here programming. All my life women have tried to pull me away from my creativity. You're a relief!"

During another computer class, when the other students were busy typing an assignment into their computers, Lance leaned over mine and typed in: "I want to make love to you."

And I typed in: "Right now? Okay, sure, why not!"

And he typed in: "This is *fun!*"

After a month Lance said, "I love you."

We were in bed at my house, about to go to sleep.

I said it right back. "I love you, too."

"Oh thank God! I was scared to tell you that. That's why I waited until it was so late. I figured I could say it and then quick fall asleep just in case you didn't say it back—at least I wouldn't know! I love you, I love you, I love you, I love you! Now good night!"

"I don't understand this man," I said to Max. "He's every alcoholic woman's dream. He says 'I love you' more than even I need to hear it. He thinks I'm beautiful. You were right, he didn't care about the age thing. (It was seven years!) He met Emily and was lovely to her. He thinks being a recovering alcoholic is great. What's the hitch?"

"Jesus, Sylvia, there you go again! If it works, don't fix it! This is what you've been working for all these years. You've paid your dues, now enjoy it. You deserve it."

"I have to tell you one of my secrets," Lance said to me one day.

Oh-oh! Here comes the hitch! He's found younger flesh; he's gay part-time; he's moving back to Denmark; he's got herpes...

210

"I have another son."

"Oh, is *that* all!"

"Michael. He'd be twenty by now. I've been married three times. His Mom was number two. She couldn't handle my wicked musician's ways. I was your basic louse. When Michael was two, she left. I tried to find them, but I never could. She married again and I don't even know what her name is."

Looking at him, I wished Emily were there to see. She probably would have said that at that very moment Lance had "watery eyes."

I leaned forward, put my arms around him, and held him tight. I wasn't the only one with wreckage behind me. I guess you don't have to be an alcoholic for that. And I wasn't the only one who didn't come with guarantees. It was possible I'd drink again. It was possible Lance would philander again.

That is, if either one of us decided that doing these things was worth the price.

"I hope you find him someday," I said.

"I do too. At least I found you."

One weekday evening I was at Lance's apartment reading a book on his bed while he was in the living room helping Alan with homework. He kept poking his head in to tell me he loved me.

"It makes me feel good seeing you there reading. I love the way you look with glasses on. How'd you like to make it a lifetime?"

Without missing a beat I said, "I would."

We were engaged.

I checked inside myself to see how I was handling it—all was calm and clear. Not a ripple of doubt. In fact, the feeling I had surprised me and made me happy. It was the feeling of "I'm home."

Everything was all so easy. Where was the drama? Where was the pain? Where was that familiar old anxiety? "I'm not in enough danger here!" I kept thinking. Where were the obstacles? Where was Lance's resistance to commitment?

Why wasn't the universe fighting me?

"This is the way it's supposed to be," said Max. "For once you're going with the flow. If you hadn't been so pokey about getting your spiritual act together, you'd know that by now. Remember in the est training when they tell you it's easier to ride a horse in the direction he's going? Well, up until now you've been trying to ride the horse the wrong way."

Max bugged me when he told me I wasn't "spiritual."

"Dammit, Max! Lance isn't spiritual either," I whined with more than a touch of my old defensiveness. "Lance is earthy. He's never meditated. He's never heard of est or zen or any of the new-age consciousness writers. Lance is all numbers and logic and computers—yet you yourself said he's a grown-up. How do you explain that?"

"He may surprise you."

Sometime later Lance and I were having one of our multi-faceted discussions. We touched briefly on the topic of soccer. Soccer was what had brought him to America when he was only sixteen.

"What got you into soccer in the first place?" I asked politely, but my smug little attitude was showing through. To me all sports were boring and a waste of time. What I really wanted to add to my question was, "Why soccer when there are so many other worthwhile things to do?"

"I always had a good eye. I could follow the ball and catch it. Some people can't. They made me a goalie."

"A good eye? I didn't know there were individual differences. How does somebody develop a good eye in sports? What do you have to do special to follow a ball with your eye and catch it?"

"I don't know what other people do, but what I did was change the speed of the ball. Whenever the ball was coming at me, I'd just look at it and in my mind I'd slow it down. Of course that way made it a lot easier to catch."

"Of course!" Then I started laughing. I couldn't help myself.

"What's funny?"

"Tell me, do you also bend spoons long distance?"

"Bend spoons? I don't get it. What do you mean, 'bend spoons'?"

"I'll tell you someday."

Lance and I were married at Christmas time in a little Connecticut-like church. Between us, we'd had five other weddings. But this was the first church wedding for both of us—we felt virginal again.

It was an evening ceremony. There were candles burning and incense and baroque music—some of my favorite things.

"It's okay to light candles?" I'd asked the minister. "I can burn incense? It's okay to have a jazz trio at the reception?" I was still surprised when I was allowed adult privileges. "I can do that?"

The minister smiled at me. He'd known me a few years. He knew what a fruitcake I'd been. "Yes, Sylvia, you can do that. It's your

212

wedding. You can do anything you want short of consummation on the altar."

I wore a borrowed off-white dress, a hot pink sash, and lacy stockings. My sister sent a huge bouquet from New York with a note: "All my single friends are here with me, cheering! Your story is an inspiration to them! We love you and wish we could be with you on this very special day. Lots of love." The flowers went on the altar.

Sandy's sister Faye sent a telegram. How strange she should hover over this wedding just like the last one. Momentarily I expected a door to slam and I'd know "Faye's rays" had struck again! I'd seen Faye a few months earlier in New York. She had never stopped drinking, but had, oddly enough, found moments of peace for herself in yoga. Sober, she was touchingly sweet to me and a doting aunt to Emily and Abby. But after a few Scotches she turned surly again. I always made it a point to mention my alcoholism and my recovery to her "in passing." I hoped she'd bite and say, "I need help."

But it never happened. In her mind, there wasn't even a problem to need help with.

I no longer saw people like Faye or my patients at the hospital as Purple Cows, as "them" that I'd rather see than be. Faye could be my clone. When I looked at Faye, I saw what might have become of me if I hadn't made that decision to stop drinking gin over twelve years ago.

"There but for the grace of God go *I*..."

Abby, home from college for Christmas, and Emily were bridesmaids.

"It's so totally weird to go to your own mother's wedding!" Abby said to me under her breath. "I feel like I haven't been born yet." Suddenly her sister caught her eye. "Emily, stop doing that!"

Emily was nervous about our upcoming walk down the aisle. She was picking the hairs out of the back of her hand again.

"Remember, honey, they can't tell you have learning disabilities," I reminded her.

She laughed right away.

"*Or* that you're an alcoholic!" she said. "*Or* that Abby sees auras!" She was getting into the game. "What does Lance do?"

"Bends spoons."

"Oh, psychic powers!" she said.

I looked at her. How the hell did she know that?

Max gave me away.

We stood just outside the rectory together waiting for the baroque music to start.

"Max, it's scary to think that if I hadn't gone to New York I wouldn't have gotten into computers. And if I hadn't gotten into computers, I wouldn't have met Lance. And if I hadn't met Lance I wouldn't be standing here right now hanging onto your arm for dear life."

"Synchronicity." He gave me a big squeezy hug just like Walt used to do. And, like Walt, he looked happy and proud of me.

The music began. Abby and Emily began their walk down the aisle ahead of us.

Max had one more thing to say: "Remember, it's okay to be happy. You *earned* it."

When we got to the altar, Lance was there—punctual as usual! He looked beautiful! God, I'm lucky! I thought.

The minister leaned forward. "Well, how do you like it so far?"

Lance and I giggled. It cured my buckling knees so I was even able to pay attention to the words.

I caught a glimpse of Mattie in the front row, tears of sheer pleasure in her eyes. She'd been through each of the many chapters with me the last few years. Now she and Max were symbolically handing me over to Lance, but in reality—to myself.

I was finally being put in charge of my own life. I'd shown I could handle it—that is, with a little help from my friends!

"Wasn't that fun!" Lance said in the car on the way home from the wedding. The back seat was full of gifts and flowers, just as it had been twenty-two years earlier when I'd married Sandy. I looked at Lance's uneven, sensuous profile and at the cigarette he held in his right hand which rested on the steering wheel—and I smiled. Another oral husband! So many things were just the same—and yet everything was different.

I thought about all those years of drinking that crazy liquid called gin and of all the damage it had done. How on earth did I get here from there? I don't know. But I know how I could get back again—take that first drink!

Some people say that sobriety is a gift, but I don't think it's a gift. Sobriety is a loan. And if I don't make my installment payments on it by doing certain things to *stay* sober, the "repo" man will appear at my door and take it away from me.

So I keep going to recovery group meetings and I do whatever else I have to do to learn the art of living, sometimes with the words of my first mentor, Pauline, still ringing in my ears: "All that's expected of you, Sylvia, is that you change absolutely everything." Or as Inez later so succinctly put it: "Become a better person—or die!"

I think I *have* become a better person—not a perfect person but a better one.

I know I'm a better therapist. Today the things I tell my patients come out of my experience, not a book. And when I talk to them about addiction I know whereof I speak—I've *been* there. And I've found that none of my experiences have been wasted, not even the bad ones. It's all grist for the mill.

Sometimes I wish I could recall all my patients issued before a certain date and have another crack at them. I hope a few of them, like poor JoLynn back at Boston State Hospital, managed to survive my "treatment" and get the help they needed!

Everything we do or don't do in life has a price tag attached. I've paid a price for my addiction, a price for my "lapses in judgment" and a price for my involvement in the adventure of women's liberation. And yet if I had it all to do over—I *would*. I feel extremely lucky to have found another loving mate after throwing the first one away so cavalierly. And I feel lucky to be back to writing again after I threw that away too. And most of all I feel lucky just to be alive. Most people who take a nose dive into addiction never pull out of it.

"We all deliver personal peace to ourselves," Aristotle said. And I agree. I feel at peace—comfortable in work, in love, and at play. And to me that's what "learning the art of living is all about."

At one of those workshops I used to attend I heard about the Myth of the Iron Wound. Apparently in olden days in Finland they believed that if you were wounded by a sword, you could heal yourself by telling the story of the history of the iron from which the sword was made. And in some ways that's what I've done here. I've played "scribe" and I've told the story of the history of my own wound.

And now I think this healer has finally been healed.

Sometimes I hate addiction and the ugly things it does to beautiful people. Addiction is "Big Brother" somebody once said. Addiction is a dirty street fighter that renders us all as helpless as uptown kids. Addiction is a siren that sings a song and for some of us, unless we tie ourselves down to the deck like Ulysses in *The Odyssey*, we'll end up following the siren song and crashing on the rocks.

215

Sometimes I'm grateful to addiction. Because of it, I was dragged kicking and screaming and with great gnashing of teeth into a happy life.

I don't know why some people can learn the art of living just by living—and others, like me, have to be clonked over the head with a bottle of gin before they become teachable.

I don't know what caused my alcoholism. The latest evidence says it's genetic but there's still no proof. I don't know what caused Emily's autism. The latest evidence says it's biochemical, but there's no proof of that either. Sometimes she asks me the impossible "Why me?" question—"Why am *I* autistic? Why do I have learning disabilities? Why am I obsessive-compulsive? (She knows all the words!) Why can't I drive a car? Why not Abby? Why *me*?" When she asks this it breaks my heart and I have to tell her I just don't know. But I also tell her that I love her very much the way she is. And I do.

I don't know why Abby can see auras and I can't or why earth-bound Lance can slow down soccer balls in mid-air with his mind and I can't.

And when it comes to healing, I don't know what cures people—of addiction or of anything else. I'm pretty sure it involves a sudden "worldview shift" (or "flash experience" as I call it.) It's something that has to happen within the person, but just what it is that triggers or ignites this flash or shift is a mystery—"Snake oil stuff, Sylvia," as Gil would have said as he puffed away on a marijuana cigarette.

Maybe, but it happens. I've seen it.

Even better, I've experienced it.

Twenty-two years ago I thought that being a therapist in the happiness business meant I was privy to the answers to life's gnarly questions. I was wrong. And what I've learned since then is there are very few answers and many, many mysteries.

I don't feel like a "victim" of anything anymore—not of addiction, not of Emily's autism, not of chauvinism, not of feminism, not even of the times. I figure every human being on earth gets an average of 3.2 tragedies per lifetime and I've just had my share, that's all. Aristotle's arrow zinged me a few times and it'll zing me again—but it missed me a few times, too.

I've had my share of the bad stuff, and I've had my share of the good stuff.

I think I prefer the good stuff.

*Do not despair—many are happy much of the time; more eat than starve, more are healthy than sick, more curable than dying; not so many dying as dead; and one of the thieves was saved. Hell's bells and all's well—half the world is at peace with itself, and so is the other half; vast areas are unpolluted; millions of children grow up without suffering deprivations, and millions, while deprived, grow up without suffering cruelties, and millions, while deprived and cruelly treated, nonetheless grow up: No laughter is sad and many tears are joyful.*

Tom Stoppard, Jumpers, *Act I*